Buddhist Economics

Buddhist Economics

*An Enlightened Approach to the
Dismal Science*

Clair Brown

BLOOMSBURY PRESS

NEW YORK · LONDON · OXFORD · NEW DELHI · SYDNEY

Bloomsbury Press
An imprint of Bloomsbury Publishing Plc

1385 Broadway   50 Bedford Square
New York   London
NY 10018   WC1B 3DP
USA   UK

www.bloomsbury.com

BLOOMSBURY and the Diana logo are trademarks of Bloomsbury Publishing Plc

This book grew out of an article originally published in 2015 in *Challenge:
The Magazine of Economic Affairs* © 2015, 2016.

First published 2017

ISBN: HB: 978-1-63286-366-9
         ePub: 978-1-63286-367-6

LIBRARY OF CONGRESS CATALOGING-IN-PUBLICATION DATA
Names: Brown, Clair, 1946- author.
Title: Buddhist economics: an enlightened approach to the dismal science /
Clair Brown.
Description: New York: Bloomsbury, 2017. | Includes bibliographical references.
Identifiers: LCCN 2016025284 | ISBN 9781632863669 (hardcover)
Subjects: LCSH: Economics—Religious aspects—Buddhism. |
Economics—Philosophy.
Classification: LCC BQ4570.E25 B76 2017 | DDC 330.1—dc23
LC record available at https://lccn.loc.gov/2016025284.

2 4 6 8 10 9 7 5 3 1

Typeset by RefineCatch Limited, Bungay, Suffolk
Printed and bound in the U.S.A. by Berryville Graphics Inc., Berryville, Virginia

To find out more about our authors and books visit www.bloomsbury.com. Here
you will find extracts, author interviews, details of forthcoming events and the
option to sign up for our newsletters.

Bloomsbury books may be purchased for business or promotional use. For
information on bulk purchases please contact Macmillan Corporate and Premium
Sales Department at specialmarkets@macmillan.com.

To my family and friends for their love and caring,
To Mother Earth for nurturing life through the ages.

CONTENTS

INTRODUCTION

ECONOMICS AFFECTS HOW we live and how happy we are. Yet most people ignore economics even though it has a powerful impact on our lives and our future.

Take our two biggest worldwide challenges: global warming and income inequality. United Nations climate scientists warn that time is running out if we are to avoid destroying our planet and our way of life. Income inequality rivals that of the Gilded Age, with economists predicting that inequality will continue to grow, along with political turmoil.

Both of these challenges are profoundly influenced by economics. Overcoming them will require a complete rethinking of our economic system, our lives, and what matters to us. We must learn to live in harmony with Nature and with one another.

I have been an economist at the University of California, Berkeley, for a lifetime and a Buddhist for a decade. As a professor of economics and a student of Buddhism, I have been grappling for some time now with the troubling disconnect between free market economics and the issues of the real world. In an era marked by vast economic disparities and the threat of environmental collapse, with opulent living for a few, comfortable living for many, and deprivation with suffering for most, something is clearly wrong.

Free market economics assumes that markets produce optimal outcomes and people have the resources to create satisfying lives. In measuring national well-being, economics focuses only on income and consumption, and excludes many of the pressing issues that define our modern life.

What would a Buddhist approach to economics, in which people are regarded as more important than output and a meaningful life is prized above a lavish lifestyle, look like? I began to wonder.

My thinking about how to reframe economics from a Buddhist perspective was inspired initially by studying Buddhism with compassionate, knowledgeable teachers at the Nyingma Institute in Berkeley. Then a Tibetan Buddhist meditation hall opened not far from our house. My husband and I stopped by and heard a talk given by Anam Thubten Rinpoche, a Tibetan Buddhist lama, and began practicing with him. As I embraced the core Buddhist concepts of interdependence, compassion, and right livelihood, I wondered, "How would Buddha teach Introductory Economics?"

Four years ago, I put my musings into action by teaching a sophomore seminar on Buddhist economics at Berkeley, in part to develop my own thinking on the subject. The students energetically engaged in addressing questions about inequality, happiness, and sustainability, teaching me what I already suspected: you don't have to be an economics major or practice Buddhism to join in the conversation about how Buddhism can connect the human spirit and the economy to create well-being and happiness for all people.

As a Buddhist and an economics professor, I join the chorus of economists asking whether there is an alternative to an economy ruled by desire and ill equipped to address the challenges of environmental deterioration, inequality, and personal suffering.

BECOMING HAPPY

What makes people happy? This question takes us to the heart of the difference between free market economics and Buddhist economics: our human nature. According to Buddhist economics, human nature is generous and altruistic, even as it also cares about itself. Buddha taught that all people suffer from their own mental states, with feelings of discontent that come from desiring more and more. The Dalai Lama tells us that the feeling of not having enough and wanting more does not arise from the inherent desirability of the objects we are seeking, but from our own mental illusions. Buddha taught us how to end suffering by changing our states of mind, which translates into finding happiness through living a meaningful life.

Free market economics holds that human nature is self-centered and that people care only about themselves as they push ahead to maximize their incomes and fancy lifestyles. According to this approach, buying and consuming—shopping for new shoes or playing a new video game—will make you happy. Forget that soon you will grow tired of the shoes, become disappointed with the game, and be off shopping again. In this endless cycle of desire, we are continuously left wanting more without ever finding lasting satisfaction. Free market economics is not guiding us toward living meaningful lives in a healthy world, nor is it offering solutions to our concerns about global wars, income equality, and environmental threats.

Buddhist economics, in contrast, provides guidance for restructuring both our individual lives and the economy to create a better world. "Practice compassion to be happy" replaces "More is better." "Everyone's well-being is connected" replaces "Maximize your own position." "The welfare of humans and Nature is interdependent" replaces "Pollution is a social cost that the individual can ignore."

NO TIME TO LOSE

Climate scientists warn that we don't have much time left to make the switch from an income-driven world with little concern for environmental harm to an economy that dramatically reduces our carbon footprint. Scientists around the world release a steady flow of reports on how human activity is causing global warming and how it harms our lives now and will into the future. Yet most people seem too busy to listen and take action.

On the same weekend in January 2015, two very different articles appeared: one, in the highly respected journal *Science*, reported that threats to our environment endanger our way of life; the other, in the *New York Times*, described the servicing of private superyachts that require professional crews and cost millions of dollars. The *Science* article reported that an international team of eighteen scientists has found that four of the nine earth biophysical processes crucial to maintaining the stability of the planet have become dangerously compromised by human activity: the systems of biosphere integrity (extinction rate), biogeochemical flows (phosphorus-nitrogen cycle), land system change (deforestation for crops and cities), and climate change (atmospheric carbon dioxide concentration). The *New York Times* article reported that more than one fifth of the estimated five thousand superyachts in the world were purchased in the last five years, during the Great Recession. I suspect that many more people paid attention to the *New York Times* article than the *Science* article; despite our knowledge about the disastrous damage that we are inflicting on the earth, consumption continues to fascinate and accelerate. Materialistic drives are pushing us toward the "sixth extinction," as many are now referring to today's ongoing extinction of species.

Inequality is equally relentless. In many economies, inequality has dramatically increased as the surge in income and wealth since the mid-1970s has been captured by the top 1 percent and done little to benefit the majority of families. Economists have warned us that inequality can slow economic growth and reduce people's sense of well-being. But during the Great Recession following the global financial crisis of 2008, ordinary people paid the price of a crisis that was caused by the powerful financial sector, which recovered just fine as a result of government bailouts. In the United States, the bailout cost taxpayers $21 billion, plus billions in lost wages.

Income inequality is not uniform across nations. Some countries (the United States, the United Kingdom, India, and China) have created much more inequality than others (including many European nations and Japan). Such inequality is not inevitable; it is a national choice that results from government policies. For example, Denmark and Sweden have a progressive tax structure and social programs that provide everyone with health care, child care, and education along with a safety net for hard times. In contrast, the United States has a much less progressive tax structure and a flimsy safety net, and private companies are in charge of much of health care and child care.

Similarly, climate scientists have demonstrated that burning fossil fuels, causing carbon dioxide emissions that heat the planet, is the result of many choices that governments make. The United States has aggravated both global warming and inequality by allowing big business, especially the fossil fuel and finance industries, to be big political players. Countries choose to institute policies that result in global warming and inequality, and they can reverse them if they so desire.

THE TERM "BUDDHIST economics" was first coined by E. F. Schumacher in his 1973 book *Small Is Beautiful: Economics as if People Mattered.* Schumacher foresaw the problems that come about with excessive reliance on the growth of income, especially overwork and dwindling resources. He argued for a system that valued individual character development and human liberation over an attachment to material goods. In Schumacher's view, the goal of Buddhist economics is "the maximum of well-being with the minimum of consumption."

My approach expands on Schumacher's notion of Buddhist economics to accommodate a world that couldn't have been envisioned in 1973, and to advocate an approach to organizing the economy so that a meaningful life reflects our caring for one another and global sharing of the world's resources in a sustainable system. Buddha taught that true happiness does not come from the external world, not from fame or consumption or friends or power. True happiness comes from within ourselves as we surrender to the great unknown, develop love and compassion for everyone, and become aware of every precious moment of life.

We are failing at both the personal and the national level, and we must wake up and take action. And we do not have to don sackcloth and stop living comfortable, interesting, and fulfilling lives to do so. We can reprogram our economic system to create, measure, and evaluate what we value, to develop well-performing economies that provide meaningful lives for everyone while protecting the planet. Buddhist economics can guide us along the way.

BUDDHIST ECONOMICS IS NOT JUST FOR BUDDHISTS (OR ECONOMISTS)

As I learned by teaching my sophomore seminar at Berkeley, you don't have to be a Buddhist to embrace a Buddhist approach to economics. You need only share the Dalai Lama's belief that human nature is gentle and compassionate and embrace the idea that economics can be a force for good, one that goes beyond self-centered materialism.

In urging kindness and compassion, Buddhism does not stand apart from other major religions. Christianity, Islam, Hinduism, and Judaism all have their own versions of the Golden Rule, "treat others as you would like others to treat you." As the Dalai Lama teaches, "Every religion emphasize[s] human improvement, love, respect for others, [and] sharing other people's suffering," with all the major religions aiming to help people achieve lasting happiness. The main difference between Buddhism and other religions is that it does not posit an external god; instead, each person is regarded as sacred, and each of us has our own inner Buddha, which is our perfect true self and an inexhaustible source of love, compassion, and wisdom.

Many people all over the world have read about or tried Buddhism, and even those who decide that the practice is not for them still likely agree with the basic principles. For example, in *The Happiness Project*, the bestselling author Gretchen Rubin writes, "I had to find some way to steer my mind toward the transcendent and the timeless, away from the immediate and the shallow . . . to appreciate the glories of the present moment . . . to put the happiness of others before my own happiness. Too often, these eternal values got lost in the hubbub of everyday routines and selfish concerns." Anyone who believes in these sorts of lessons, and approaches life with an open heart and an inquiring mind, can benefit from Buddhist economics.

Being interdependent with one another and with Nature does not mean uniformity of action, or conformity. We don't have to give up our unique personalities, which help us navigate life in the external world. Rather, being connected means being mindful of each precious moment in life, as well as mindful of our feelings and our impact on others. In Buddhism, we want to be in touch with our true nature so that we are not driven by our ego, which plays and replays our daily habits of fear, guilt, shame, greed, jealousy, hatred . . . the list goes on and on. Our continual judgment of ourselves and others, our attachment to possessions and relationships with continual longing for more, our ignorance of the suffering we are causing others and Nature by our lifestyle—all cause pain and make us unhappy. But if we know ourselves and are aware of the people and world around us in each moment throughout the day, then our regrets about the past and our worries about the future dissolve. We awaken to the magic of the moment and find happiness as our suffering ends.

When we are feeling discontented in our egocentric materialistic world, we use strategies that bring momentary distraction and maybe even brief periods of happiness. We may go shopping for new clothes, or play a new game on our iPhone, or stream a favorite television show. In a Buddhist world, in contrast, a person experiencing pain may sit quietly to let go of the feelings and illusions causing the pain, or talk to a friend who understands the pain, or enjoy a family meal. Instead of escaping the feeling of unhappiness or discontent, a person is mindful of what is happening and finds ways to enjoy what is meaningful in life. Each moment is too precious to waste in self-made pain, and we can use awareness to enjoy life to the fullest without relying on consumerism.

PRACTICING MINDFULNESS

On a personal level, many people benefit from mindfulness practice, which is being aware of the moment without judgment while you relax your body, quiet your mind, and open your heart. Usually people practice mindfulness while sitting in a chair or on a cushion. Others find that walking slowly, or practicing yoga, or shooting archery, allows them to live fully in the present moment.

In this millennium, mindfulness sitting has taken the country by storm. We see mindfulness meditation headlines on the covers of magazines ranging from *Parade* (2015) and *Time*

In my Buddhist economics seminar, we sit for five to ten
minutes at each class, and the students think the mindfulness
sitting is one of our deepest lessons. I suggest that they practice
sitting quietly whenever they find themselves in a stressful situation, to quiet their minds so that they can ease their pain and
think more clearly.

As the class deadline for turning in their journals approached,
a student named Joan wrote me a long email about her computer
woes and ended with, "I'm sort of freaking out and wanted to
see if it would be all right if I sent you my journal folder a little
later today. Like I said, I have them. I just need to get a new
charger before I can send them in!"

I responded,

Relax, breathe
and know you will be ok.
Fine to turn in journal once computer is working.

Joan wrote back, "Right after emailing you I remembered
you telling us to meditate, take five, and sit after something
stressful happens. I did and man I felt better!"

On a personal note, I sit daily for twenty to thirty minutes.
Sitting helps me get in touch with myself and shake off my
relentless ego and judgmental thoughts, and the stress and pain
that go with them. Sitting provides a time for my mind to rest
and restores my balance. Try it yourself. Begin by sitting five to
ten minutes each day. See how you feel and function. Once
you have learned to relax and quiet your mind, you can sit on
the subway or on the beach, along a pathway in a park, or at
home—anywhere.

(2014) to *National Geographic* (2005) and *Scientifi*
Mindfulness meditation is lauded by a Harvard
newsletter and has been shown to increase bra
have other health benefits. The Greater Good Sc
UC Berkeley has produced a couple of short, spi
show how meditation changes your brain so you
Watch them if you want inspiration. Many peopl
that practicing mindfulness sitting makes them ha
feel less like a separate self and more interconnect
world as they shift from "me to we," and as they see
beliefs do not represent true reality.

Certain studies have shown that monks' meditation
have changed the way their brains function, as brain a
the right insula and both sides of their anterior c
cortices has increased. Other studies have observed that
plasticity occurred, meaning that long-term Buddhist r
tors have altered the structure as well as function o
brains.

Mindfulness meditation lessons are taught in many fe
for a wide array of prices. But you don't have to leave hon
try mindfulness sitting. Find a comfortable chair or cush
and sit quietly with your back straight and your hands in y
lap or on your knees. Focus on your breath as it flows into yc
nostrils. Relax your shoulders and feel your entire body relax
you focus on your breath. Let go of your thoughts. If a though
arises, let it pass by without following it, without judging it. Si
quietly and let your illusions about life dissolve. Let go of any
regrets about the past, for yesterday is over. Let go of your
relentless to-do list, for the future has not arrived. Enjoy the
preciousness of the moment. Sink deeply into the peacefulness.

LET'S JOIN TOGETHER IN CREATING CHANGE

Many people want to live more meaningful lives and want to take action to save the planet. What is holding us back?

I see three main forces getting in our way:

First, our "busyness." None of us has enough time to do all the things on our to-do list. Work, family, friends, community are all important to us, and they demand our time and talent and drain our energy. I hope this book will help you think about how to get off the treadmill and focus in a meaningful way on the things that are truly important to you.

Second, our denial. Moving from free market economics to Buddhist economics takes courage and determination. Learning how to live a meaningful life undermines many people's sense of a successful life. Addressing climate change threatens two concepts many people hold dear: free markets and unending progress. Denial of the problems is one way to live with them, but it doesn't work in the long run.

Third, our ignorance. Waking up to the toll of the treadmill, and to how our lifestyle is harming others and killing the planet, requires that we educate ourselves and change the way we live. This is a big deal, but it is our moral responsibility, both to ourselves and to others. Buddhist economics tells us that in so doing, we will become happier.

These forces may also get in the way of your reading this book. You may be too busy to read it, much less to think about what is important to you and put steps in place to restructure your life. You may think that free market economics has it right and throw this book against the wall. You may like living in ignorance, preferring to leave the saving of the planet to others while you live a life where external status, filled with lots of stuff, plays a major part.

But you may also be looking for something more. I have met many people who are already on the path to living meaningful lives in harmony with Nature. This book is written for them, as well as for those who want to learn more about this path. It is within our power to go beyond consumption, to be connected to others with compassion, and to exist in harmony with Nature. Let us begin.

Chapter 1

WHY WE NEED A HOLISTIC
ECONOMIC MODEL

There are many examples in the modern world showing how this doctrine of the free market—the pursuit of self-interest—has worked out to the disadvantage of society.

—CAMBRIDGE PROFESSOR JOAN ROBINSON, 1977

The approach used here concentrates on a factual basis that differentiates it from more traditional practical ethics and economic policy analysis, such as the "economic" concentration on the primacy of income and wealth (rather than on the characteristics of human lives and substantive freedoms).

—NOBEL LAUREATE AMARTYA SEN,
DEVELOPMENT AS FREEDOM

WHAT MAKES LIFE worth living? Ask economists, and their answers will depend on their view of how the economy works, and on their criteria for evaluating economic performance. In free market economic models, a person's well-being is measured by "utility" (satisfaction), which is in turn measured by income, and a country's well-being is measured by its market output or total income. The free market judges a country's performance by how fast its income is growing, but it ignores the distribution of income within that country.

In Buddhist economics, people are interdependent with one another and with Nature, so each person's well-being is measured by how well everyone and the environment are functioning with the goal of minimizing suffering for people and the planet. Everyone is assumed to have the right to a comfortable life with access to basic nutrition, health care, education, and the assurance of safety and human rights. A country's well-being is measured by the aggregation of the well-being of all residents and the health of the ecosystem.

In simplest terms, the free market model measures prosperity by focusing on growth in average income per person and in national output, while the Buddhist model measures prosperity by focusing on the quality of life of all people and Nature.

This straightforward answer doesn't take into consideration the usual caveats that accompany economic explanations. For a deeper understanding, we need to compare these two approaches and how each assumes the world works.

The free market model assumes that markets are competitive and that they work flawlessly to produce optimal social outcomes: People are rational decision makers with perfect information. Firms do not have the market power to set prices, so profits cannot rise above a low competitive level. Markets set prices, so supply equals demand, and national economies hum along with no excess profits, no underutilized labor or capital; everyone is treated fairly.

These assumptions are based on the belief that people spend their money wisely and are satisfied with their purchases. Whatever an individual chooses to buy is optimal because only that person knows what is best for her. The free market model puts a high premium on individualism and self-centered freedom, and on buying more and more. Have another drink, buy another pair of shoes, play another electronic game, eat fast food for dinner, do whatever you want to do. "Impulse buying," such as grabbing things off the shelf when we are hungry and/or buying something that we see advertised online with a click, is as rational as any other decision. People are not swayed in the moment by advertising or a bad day at the office, because the assumption is that they are consistent in their values and wise in their decisions.

In addition, free market economics doesn't care about inequality, and it ignores the well-being of the people who do not have money to "vote" in the marketplace. Markets can only distribute goods and services to people with money to spend. Poor people are excluded from participating in many markets, while rich people dominate markets because they dominate consumption. No matter how much someone values something, such as eating fresh fruit or seeing a doctor, they can only have it if they can pay for it.

We know that Buddhist economics and free market economics use very different criteria for judging proposed economic policies to improve social well-being. Free market economics uses a simple rule called *Pareto optimality*, which denotes an economic state in which it is impossible to make one person better off without making at least one other person worse off. A proposed policy passes the Pareto improvement test if some people gain and nobody loses. In stark contrast, Buddhist economics strives for a holistic optimal outcome and evaluates a policy by how much it minimizes suffering. By reducing the suffering of people living impoverished and bleak lives, we improve the well-being of everyone.

Income transfers from the rich to the poor do not improve economic outcomes in the free market model, thus a dollar transferred from the billionaire Bill Gates to the hungry child Jane is not a Pareto improvement. Jane is better off, but Bill is worse off. Spending by the rich adds as much to social welfare as spending by the poor.

In the Buddhist economic model, however, transfers of income from the rich to the poor improve economic outcomes because the well-being of everyone is interconnected. More income to the poor helps them buy basic goods and services, which relieves suffering and also improves their health, educational attainment, and lifetime outcomes for the children, while the rich reduce the consumption of luxuries that separates them from others; everyone's well-being improves. Philosopher Peter Singer advocates global transfers by arguing that buying luxuries cannot be justified if the money could be used to save a person's life.

The free market model, the focus of the Chicago school of economists, dominated economic thinking from the 1970s through the end of the twentieth century. Questions of equity and justice were pushed to the back burner (or to the field of sociology). After all, free market economics argues that any interference in "free" competitive markets only makes society worse off. Economics focused primarily on maximizing average income while ignoring issues of equity and justice.

Conservative politicians today still tout the free market model, and students still learn it in Introductory Economics. But economists have moved away from it and use a variety of models with more realistic worldviews, including models with a renewed focus on economic justice.

Today, morality in economics is returning from a half-century hiatus, and research on inequality, poverty, and discrimination is taking center stage again. In pathbreaking work, some of the world's top economists, such as George Akerlof, Angus Deaton, Paul Krugman, Thomas Piketty, Emmanuel Saez, Amartya Sen, and Joseph Stiglitz, argue for policies to create more equitable, just, and sustainable economic systems. Anthony Atkinson, Samuel Bowles, and Jeffrey Sachs explicitly argue for incorporating morality into economics and explain how to do it.

Buddhist economics is built upon these broader models, including those known as *asymmetric information* (information is not perfect), *behavioral economics* (consumers are not "rational" decision makers), *relative income* (individual preferences depend on social norms and the comparing of one's income to others' income), *altruism* (people care about what happens to others), *market failures* (firms don't pay for pollution, and most industries are not competitive but are controlled by a few firms), *human capabilities* (people's ability to function in their daily lives determines their well-being), and *moral hazard* (financial firms reap profits without bearing the risk of failure).

The Buddhist model builds upon these extensions of economics to end up with very different outcomes and policies from the free market model. In fact, Buddhist economics is diametrically opposed to the free market model in explaining how the economy delivers prosperity, justice, and sustainability. Once we move beyond the notion that no matter what we have, we want more, and getting more is always good, we can measure economic performance holistically. Buddhist economics takes into consideration the protection of the environment, the state of the human spirit, and the quality of life of all people. Once we start to measure economic growth to incorporate these values, we will have new measures of wellbeing to guide us in changing the world.

Most likely this book won't have enough rigor for some economists or enough dharma for some Buddhists. But I am not writing this book for them. Drawing upon the best economic thinking and Buddhist teachings being done today, my goal is to expand the dialogue among people around the world who seek meaningful lives for all, on a planet with thriving ecosystems.

Hopefully people from all walks of life and disciplines will add to this dialogue of how to create a global economy that provides prosperity, equity, and sustainability and ends suffering. No matter whether you are Christian, Jewish, Hindu, Muslim or some other religion or atheist, read along with me and think about how economics can help make life more meaningful, just, and sustainable.

May we all live together with prosperity and compassion in harmony with Nature.

Chapter 2

WHAT IS BUDDHIST ECONOMICS?

> *Ideally, economics should play a part in providing
> [humankind] with opportunities for real individual
> and social growth rather than simply being a tool for
> catering to selfish needs and feeding contention in
> society, and, on a broader scale, creating imbalance
> and insecurity within the whole global structure with
> its innumerable ecosystems.*
>
> *Our ethics—and the behaviour that naturally flows
> from our ethics—contribute to the causes and condi-
> tions that determine who we are, the kind of society we
> live in and the condition of our environment.*
>
> —PAYUTTO, *BUDDHIST ECONOMICS*

At the outset, let's confront the perplexing problem of how to integrate the spiritual approach of Buddhism with the intellectual approach of economics. Indeed, the very term "Buddhist economics" is oxymoronic. Buddhism is spiritual, not conceptual, and economics is a system of concepts.

The Buddhist distinction between relative and ultimate truth can provide a way around this conundrum. As Khyentse Rinpoche teaches, relative truth covers the daily practices of mindfulness, nonviolence, meditation, vegetarianism, and many others, while ultimate truth is beyond conceptualization and cannot be described. Relative truths are useful in daily life, even if they are not the ultimate truth, and studying them can be very helpful. In this book, I use relative truths as our Buddhist guide in daily life.

THE THREE ELEMENTS OF A BUDDHIST APPROACH TO ECONOMICS

The core Buddhist teaching used in setting up an economic system is *interdependence*. Buddhism teaches that we are all one, and that our interdependence extends to Nature and all beings. Interdependence provides the path for leading happy lives as individuals, as well as for creating policies to support a prosperous and sustainable life for everyone. We all share the same basic motivation—to be happy—and this makes us alike and equal.

Interdependence in Buddhist economics is expressed in three ways. The first involves using resources to enhance the quality of life for ourselves and for others. The second integrates caring for Nature and our environment into all activities. And the third involves reducing suffering and practicing compassion, both locally and globally.

The first interdependence emphasizes overcoming one's self (our ego) and the self's need to maximize its own well-being (i.e., selfishness), which is at the heart of free market economics. Other Eastern philosophies, such as Hinduism, also emphasize universal connectedness and overcoming one's mental construct of a separate self. Some Western philosophical approaches, including those of Hume and Nietzsche, share a compatible view of no separate self or a minimal concept of self as well.

The second interdependence involves being connected to our environment. Our interdependence with Nature leads us to measure the value of all the resources we use, as well as any damage we do to the environment, both right now and into the future. We harm ourselves when we harm our environment. Pollution is no longer considered a "free good" as it is in free market economics, where people and companies do not have to pay to pollute the air or water or land.

In 1971, a founder of modern ecology, Barry Commoner, expressed this interdependence as one of the four laws of ecology: "Everything is connected to everything else. There is one ecosphere for all living organisms and what affects one, affects all."

Being interconnected with our environment provides a different economic valuation than does traditional cost-benefit analysis for policies that reduce carbon dioxide emissions, protect endangered species, or preserve rivers, lakes, and groundwater. Free market economics assumes that environmental damage of all sorts is acceptable as long as the benefit to people is at least as large as the cost. Future generations are not provided a voice, except to the extent that people today want to include the value of the damage to people in the future in the cost calculation. However, people tend to be shortsighted and averse to paying for public goods, and so we usually undervalue the benefits, and overestimate the costs, of protecting the environment. This biases the economic analyses in favor of damming rivers, polluting bays, pouring carbon dioxide into the atmosphere, and destroying coral reefs.

In Buddhist economics, in contrast, we regard future generations as being as important as we are, as are natural ecosystems such as an unpolluted atmosphere and biodiversity. To put it in economic language, the Buddhist model states that Nature's ecosystems require *strong sustainability* and must be protected. Free market economics uses *weak sustainability*, which assumes that use of natural resources (natural capital) is interchangeable with the use of machines (man-made capital) or human capital in the production process. This shortsighted approach can lead to ecological disaster.

The third interdependence of Buddhist economics connects the suffering of one person to the suffering of all people. This circle of suffering includes people you have never met, even though you may wear the clothes, eat the food, or play on the devices they made. No longer is "out of sight, out of mind" an excuse for paying a pittance for high-tech running shoes made by a ten-year-old girl working ten-hour days in a Chinese factory. Now we must care about the suffering of extremely poor families who lack the basics required to be healthy and live comfortable lives, no matter if they live across town or halfway around the world.

Interdependence provides us with powerful mandates. We no longer see ourselves as separate beings and no longer strive to maximize our own well-being. We find freedom from our own suffering, and we help to relieve the suffering of others. The personal is connected to the national and global. Individual and community goals merge into the one goal of promoting the well-being of all.

This all sounds idealistic and out of reach. Can we really find a way to sync Buddhist economics with our materialistic culture? Can we really restructure our economic system in such a way that it embraces new values? My answer to both questions is yes. Throughout this book, I focus both on the individual level of Buddhist economics: how we can create meaningful and happy lives for ourselves; and on the societal level: how our governments can support policies that benefit everyone in a sustainable way.

Buddhist economics wants to move economics beyond being the "dismal science." Thomas Carlyle coined that term in 1849, and it has endured through the ages to indicate that economics is the science of scarcity, where few people satisfy their wants or even their basic needs. And indeed, our global economy does provide too little for most people, along with extravagant lifestyles for a few. But it doesn't need to be that way. Our global economy can, and should, provide prosperity, justice, and sustainability with happiness for everyone.

HAPPINESS

We all want to be happy! Yet as we wander through life searching for happiness, we feel overwhelmed by the demands of our jobs, families, and friends. We worry about how we look, fret over mistakes we just made, while our endless to-do lists roll through our minds. Worry, fret, regret.

Why is happiness so hard to find? Many of us are not even sure whether long-lasting happiness is possible, because feeling happy seems so fleeting. It comes and goes.

Happiness in free market economics means personal pleasure

and the avoidance of pain. The focus is on making yourself happy by pursuing money and buying things that make you feel good, at least in the moment. This *hedonic happiness* is measured by one's subjective judgment of life satisfaction right now.

Buddhist economics takes a different approach. It shares the view of Aristotle, who held that happiness comes from self-realization and living a worthy and moral life. This *eudaimonic happiness*, as it is known, is based on people developing their full potential and living a life in service to others and the community. Aristotle teaches us, "He is happy who lives in accordance with complete virtue and is sufficiently equipped with external goods, not for some chance period but throughout a complete life." He also says, "The contemplative life is happiest."

Buddha taught how to relieve suffering, our own and that of others, and the Dalai Lama translated this into the art of living a meaningful, joyful life. The Dalai Lama warned that material gain is based on an erroneous assumption that what we buy "can by itself alone, provide us with all the satisfaction we require," and wrote that "genuine happiness is characterized by inner peace and arises in the context of our relationships with others."

In Buddhist economics, people strive to act ethically, which requires not ruining others' experiences or even their expectations of happiness. For example, you cause harm when your words or actions anger others, or make them feel guilt, fear, shame, greed, or other mental poisons (called *klesha*s in Buddhism).

Hedonic happiness fits in well with our materialistic, goal-oriented economy. We chase our dreams of large wealth or great power or awesome sex or a major championship in the belief that they will bring us lasting happiness. Our purchase, or promotion, or love affair gives us a high. Yet that high soon wears off, and we are off chasing the next high. Our mental habits make us unhappy and discontented with life, and our minds are taken over by the "five *kleshas*": desire or attachment, hatred or aggression, delusion, pride, and envy.

Finding inner happiness is one of the goals of Buddhist economics. Buddhism holds that we attain true freedom and peace only when we quit our mental habits of reacting with cravings for external stimuli ("I've got to own that!" "Win this game!" "Earn the top spot!") and reacting with aversion to external forces ("I can't stand that!" "Defeat it!" "Get rid of it!"). Instead, Buddhism states, quiet your mind: notice the beauty as you go for a walk, enjoy your food as you eat, connect more intimately with your friends.

Our attitude toward pain illuminates the difference between the two approaches to happiness. To achieve hedonic happiness, we must avoid pain, and so we shop or drink to push away pain. Buddhist economics recognizes that pain is part of life, and that what is important is how we react to painful events, be it a minor cut with a kitchen knife or the death of someone we love. Buddhist practitioners go even further and view pain as a way to practice and cultivate mindfulness, the state of being aware of the moment and enjoying it without making judgments.

The Buddhist scripture "Two Arrows Sutra" shows us how to respond to pain in a mindful way. An arrow hits us and causes us physical or mental pain. If we react by becoming distraught and lamenting that pain, we are hit by a second arrow, this one of mental pain. The second arrow has been created by our own negative reaction, which caused us more pain. But if our response to the first arrow is to remain patient and calm, there will be no second arrow. As the great teacher Shantideva wrote,

If there's a remedy when trouble strikes,
What reason is there for dejection?
And if there is no help for it,
What use is there in being glum?

I'll not fret about such things,
To do so only aggravates my trouble.

Buddhist economics ascribes nothing intrinsically ennobling to suffering. We gain nothing directly from suffering or from feeling guilty. We can always learn from our experiences and make amends if we have harmed someone, which is a noble act and brings us happiness.

INDIVIDUAL BEHAVIOR IN BUDDHIST ECONOMICS

Buddha's Four Noble Truths guide individual behavior in Buddhist economics. Buddha explained that (1) all beings suffer; (2) our suffering comes from our ignorance and desires; (3) we can end our suffering; and (4) the Eightfold Path provides a way to live without suffering. Buddha noted that people suffer need-lessly because they are disconnected from their true nature, and that people can end their suffering by giving up their sense of separateness and their delusions.

The Eightfold Path includes three interrelated activities that directly involve economic activities: right action, right livelihood, and right effort. Because each activity in the circular Eightfold Path supports the other seven, all activities are part of our daily life. Here is how the three economic activities work together: *right action* means to do everything with mindfulness and compassion, without harming ourselves or others; this goes with *right livelihood*, earning a living without harming others while nurturing our good qualities; and these are part of *right effort*, which develops our wholesome qualities such as generosity, loving kindness, and wisdom and stamps out our unwholesome, and opposite, qualities (greed, anger, and ignorance).

Our individual personalities and lifestyles still have a place in Buddhist economics, as long as we include caring about others and relieving suffering in our daily activities, sharing our good fortune rather than becoming attached to our material possessions. Instead of rushing about buying things to achieve ephemeral happiness, we stop to look at the shells on the beach, enjoy the wildflowers in the spring fields, watch the dogs running around our neighborhood, savor the colors and shapes galore! We enjoy listening to and playing music. We paint or sculpt ceramic art for our homes. We cook delicious meals for family and friends. Human nature includes both self-regarding (egocentric and taking care of oneself) and other-regarding (altruistic and taking care of others) impulses. Opinions abound as to what degree human nature is egocentric and to what degree altruistic. Economists tend to assume human nature is self-interested, yet Bowles argues that humans developed cooperative instincts with moral sentiments over time to ensure group survival. We don't have to agree to what extent humans act out of self-interest or moral sentiment. What matters is that we agree that people have the desire, and responsibility, to take care of both themselves and others. We can make a living, even prosper, but not at the expense of others or the planet.

In Buddhism, you can enjoy your own unique personality without becoming overcome by self-imposed negative feelings that cloud your mind and cause you pain, making you say and do things you later regret. These mental habits not only make us unhappy, they also sow social discord that harms those around us. The Buddhist way of handling negativity is to sit mindfully, to allow thoughts and feelings to come and go without getting caught up and distracted by them. We become more aware of the beauty of the present moment, and quit madly worrying about the future or beating ourselves up about the past. With practice, we become more mindful throughout the day in all our activities.

In Buddhist economics, we discriminate between real happiness built upon a fully developed mindful life, and temporary happiness built around money and never-ending desires. Because the goal in Buddhist economics is to minimize the suffering of all beings, we do not aim to maximize our own income, because we want to ensure the happiness and well-being of all people.

What does this mean for your approach to life? No longer do you fill your closets and home with all kinds of stuff, no longer do you rush off to the mall or scroll through online shops when you are feeling low. In my Buddhist economics class, students explored how to apply consuming less in their own lives, because they liked shopping occasionally and wondered how to buy fewer things without feeling deprived. One student's approach was to have fun looking at shoes on sale, and felt great about not buying another pair to toss in her closet. Another student, who celebrates payday by shopping, bought a bottle of special nail polish instead of an outfit. We stop buying things we don't need and barely use, and move from a closetful (free market) to a mindful (Buddhist) approach to life. You can still be happy with new purchases and enjoy material things, but you are no longer attached to them. Consumption becomes only one aspect of your multifaceted life.

If you have taken Introductory Economics, you might ask, "Is Buddhist economics a microeconomic approach (focused on the individual and the firm) or a macroeconomic approach (focused on the national economy)?" In Buddhist economics, the micro and macro are interconnected and come together to create a high quality of life. Individuals pursue happiness for both themselves and all people, and this mindful pursuit leads to national well-being in a sustainable world.

COMMUNITY AND NATIONAL APPROACHES

In Buddhist economics, prosperity is not equated with market goods and services (gross domestic product) as in free market economics, where activities are ignored unless they include a purchase of some sort. Having dinner with family and friends, sitting quietly to enjoy our surroundings, reading a good book— the free market values these activities by the goods and services purchased, not by how much we are enjoying the experience.

In Buddhist economics, income is just one element used to measure a person's prosperity. More important is how a person is able to use resources to create a meaningful life. Central to creating a meaningful life are a person's "capabilities," that is, to what extent people are able to achieve the kind of lives they value, and how well they function on a daily basis. The capabilities of a family include their health, education, consumption of basics (such as food, shelter, and transportation), and other goods and activities that make their days interesting, comfortable, and safe, as well as their ability to participate freely in community and national life. Our capabilities support the development of our relationships, talents, and full potential.

To evaluate how a national economy is performing in Buddhist economics, we look at the distribution of well-being across its population, including equal access to opportunity. The country's institutions and services promote people's functioning in daily life and provide a safety net and security. The model also considers quality of life in terms of the ecosystem legacy that the society will pass on to future generations, including the remediation of pollution and environmental deterioration.

Let us apply the story of the two arrows to a national economy. The first powerful arrow of profit motivation in free markets is launched, and though it makes a few people rich, it harms many people and the environment. The second arrow hits people as they work hard to earn enough money to buy lots of goodies, only to find fleeting happiness on a treadmill that won't stop. People then begin to look closely at the first arrow, questioning the viability of an economy run by competition for profit. And as they come to understand the limits of free market economics, they stop shooting the second arrow at themselves and begin to develop and practice Buddhist economics. No longer is the pursuit of income the only goal. Now the "pursuit of happiness" means creating meaningful lives for everyone within a healthy ecosystem. A Buddhist economy can improve the lives of all people, even the archers of the first arrows.

National economies are integrated into the global economy, and here again free market economics and Buddhist economics take us down different paths. Free market economics teaches us that international trade can result only in higher incomes for all countries, with no country losing. This outcome is based on the concept of "comparative advantage," where differences in two countries' resources and capital supposedly result in their using different ways of producing specific goods, which provides a basis for specialization in production that results in higher national incomes for both countries through trade. For example, an industrialized country makes capital-intensive machines and trades with an emerging country that makes labor-intensive fabrics and sews clothes, and both profit.

This model may have worked well at one time, but in today's highly mechanized modern global economy, many countries use the same capital, automated methods, and computer applications, even when labor is cheap. Using the same automated production processes eliminates much of the cost advantages of specialization because now labor is a small part of the cost of production. Developing countries face markets already dominated by the industrialized world. Any gains from trade reflect the countries' global bargaining power, and once again the power of the rich dominates the power of the poor. As a result, we observe cases where incomes fall in a developing country after the country has signed a free trade agreement with the United States, as happened in Mexico under NAFTA in the 1990s.

The use of energy highlights the differences between free market economics and Buddhist economics. Although most economists favor a tax on pollution, the free market to produce and consume fossil fuels does not require energy companies to pay for the air pollution and additional environmental degradation that result from extracting oil and coal. As a result, the energy prices charged to consumers do not include environmental costs, and people overconsume gas and oil. Also, in spite of the lip service given to competition in the free market economy, the energy industry is not competitive. In 2014 five of the six largest companies in the global Fortune 500 were petroleum companies, topped only by Walmart at the number 1 spot. The energy companies have used their control over prices and costs to earn high profits, which are close to $100 billion annually, with profit margins around 25 percent. They then use these enormous profits to lobby Congress for special tax breaks and favorable regulations, which make their profits rise even higher. Because consumers do not have to pay for the CO_2 emissions caused by their driving, many Americans buy gas-guzzling SUVs and pickup trucks, in spite of the harm they are doing to the atmosphere as they drive their cars an average of more than twelve thousand miles each year.

In Buddhist economics, the full price of all resources used is included in the market prices for all goods and services. The price of gas includes a pollution tax, often called a carbon tax, equal to the cost to society of the damage done to the environment by gas consumption. Equally important, driving a car with poor gas mileage is frowned upon because of the harm it is doing to the earth. Instead of buying gas guzzlers, people are happy to own cars that are energy efficient and less polluting. Owning an electric car shows you care about climate change, and people driving Hummers are viewed askance. People are mindful of how much they drive and find ways to reduce their mileage, including carpooling, taking public transit, and picking up bread or milk for a neighbor when making a run to the grocery store. The national carbon tax can be used to develop new forms of sustainable energy, expand the public transportation system, or provide other public goods for everyone's benefit.

Notice that in this example, we have not relied on multinational companies to change their focus on profit maximization. Rather, the oil companies must now pay for their carbon pollution. The government no longer gives them tax breaks, and it closely regulates the extraction of fossil fuels that degrade the environment. Thus new competition from renewable energy companies will grow; most likely, the large oil companies themselves will push ahead in their development of renewable energy sources. Now markets are providing the correct incentives to consumers and companies to speed up the shift from fossil fuels to renewable energy, which is exactly what our planet requires.

The supply and demand curves of the marketplace, which determine prices and output, reflect our values and our customs as well as our government's role and institutions. In Buddhist economics, markets move to new prices and outputs that reflect our new interdependent values. This is a critical point in understanding the power of Buddhist economics: the new market outcomes now reflect how people want to live in a meaningful way.

OUTER AND INNER WEALTH

As you probably suspect, "wealth" means different things in the free market model and in the Buddhist model. Both include

"outer wealth," which is material-based and includes our
assets—real estate (residence, vacation home, rental property),
retirement funds, stocks and bonds, automobiles—minus our
liabilities, or what we owe to others (mortgages, loans, credit
card debt). Free market economics regards outer wealth as the
only kind of wealth, and so we are used to thinking of wealth
strictly in monetary terms.

From a social viewpoint, the distribution of wealth in the
world has become more and more unequal, and this inequality
has both people and nations concerned. In 2014, less than 1.0
percent of people, the world's superrich, owned 48 percent of
global wealth. Most of the people in the world, the bottom 80
percent, shared only 5.5 percent of global wealth. In the United
States, the top 0.1 percent (yes, one tenth of 1 percent) owned
22 percent of the nation's total wealth, or as much wealth as
owned by the bottom 90 percent of families.

Buddhist economics distinguishes between outer (material)
wealth and inner (spiritual) wealth. In Buddhism, the wealth of
human beings is intrinsic and includes our capacity to appreciate our experiences and relationships and life as it unfolds
around us. Buddhist wealth includes our mindful use of
resources to enjoy life and to help others, and Buddhism teaches
that our true wealth—love, compassion, and wisdom—is inexhaustible. Buddhism does not prohibit being wealthy in the
material sense, as long as we do not become attached to material possessions or monetary wealth of any kind, and we share
our riches with others.

The cultivation of inner wealth in Buddhism is part of a
follower's daily practice on the path to enlightenment. We can
quiet our minds and let go of our sense of a separate self and our

illusions about reality constructed by society. Our true self is like a sun that has been covered by clouds of delusion, and once we let go of our attachment to self-importance and ego and embrace our impermanence and our oneness with others and the earth, our suffering ends.

Chapter 3

INTERDEPENDENT WITH ONE ANOTHER

Since I and other beings both,
In wanting happiness, are equal and alike,
What difference is there to distinguish us,
That I should strive to have my bliss alone?

Since I and other beings both,
In fleeing suffering, are equal and alike,
What difference is there to distinguish us,
That I should save myself and not the others?
—SHANTIDEVA, *THE WAY OF THE BODHISATTVA*

BUDDHA TAUGHT THAT we are all interdependent. Visualize this by imagining Indra's Jewel Net, a net stretched to infinity in all directions, each knot containing a perfect, brilliant jewel. Every jewel reflects every other jewel, and so each reflection bears the image of all the other jewels. Whatever affects one jewel affects all jewels.

Interdependence changes how we think about who gets what, and moves us from the free market zero-sum approach, where additional resources to one person must come from another person, to a collective approach, where everyone's well-being is connected. In Buddhist economics, even when total resources remain the same, the well-being of everyone improves when we transfer resources from those who consume much more than is required to live comfortably to those who are impoverished. The economic distinction between micro (individual behavior) and macro (national outcomes) dissolves, because now individual well-being is no longer distinct from societal well-being. In a world that is constantly changing and in which everything is impermanent, it is liberating to be released from incessant worries about having more and competing with others to move ahead.

Buddhist economics assumes that people are altruistic; we want to help others and relieve their suffering without any gain to ourselves. In this way, Buddhist economics shares the concerns of economists such as Samuel Bowles and Herbert Gintis, who have analyzed the evolution of altruism and reciprocity across societies. Their book *A Cooperative Species* shows how cooperation helps societies survive and grow. They use a variety of data over thousands of years to argue that groups with cooperative, ethical norms survived and expanded, and these prosocial motivations resulted in people today being genuinely concerned about others. In *The Moral Economy*, Bowles shows how economic policies that use monetary punishments in situations where people are acting ethically rather than selfishly can result in unwanted selfish behavior. An example that may resonate for many of us is when a daycare center imposed a fine on parents who arrived late to pick up their children. Parents then thought that paying to be late made it okay, and parental tardiness increased. The economic penalty replaced the need to be a good citizen.

When psychologists study what makes people happy, they find that being kind to others makes people happier. People build upon moments of compassion because there is a positive feedback loop: when you do a kind deed (take your mom to lunch), you become happier, which makes it more likely that you will do another kind act (help your neighbor carry in groceries). Kindness makes you happier, and happier people engage in more acts of kindness. This echoes the Dalai Lama's teaching that happiness comes from practicing compassion.

Buddhist economics focuses on activities and experiences that don't have a price tag. Once our basic needs are satisfied, we evaluate our consumption in terms of how it enables us to fulfill our human potential and the quality of life. Our social and creative activities allow us to enjoy life, and the more we enjoy life, the more the idea of using consumption to distinguish oneself becomes silly (or worse).

BECOMING HAPPY

The interdependence of Buddhist economics requires that each person first learn compassion and kindness by looking inward and becoming connected to her Buddha, or true nature. We learn that happiness comes from within ourselves and not from the external world. Once you transform your own life, then you can have a positive impact on others, and the distinction between personal benefit and social benefit dissolves.

Let us see how this plays out in the real world.

Harry, a UC Berkeley student, was goal driven and very competitive in pursuing his goals. The only problem was that

Harry felt his life lacked meaning. His only happiness came from pursuing a goal, such as earning a top grade or winning a debate, and each success was followed by a depressing letdown. Harry's friend Nancy, who was taking my Buddhist economics class, saw how unhappy Harry was and suggested mindfulness sitting. Harry made fun of it as a waste of time, asking, "What is the goal?"

To get Harry interested, Nancy challenged him, saying "See if you can sit thirty minutes without having any thoughts." Harry was willing to take this challenge and even made a bet with Nancy that when he succeeded, she would take him out for a fancy dinner. Once he began sitting, however, he could not believe how hard it was to keep his mind from endless chatter, bringing up all the things he needed to do or reminding him of times when others had outperformed him. Sitting felt torturous, both physically and mentally. He decided that he had to begin by practicing at least twice a day for a few minutes to build up his time. The first two weeks were the hardest, and he almost gave up, but he could not bear the thought of confessing failure to Nancy. After a month, he was doing a bit better and realized he needed a teacher. He began going to a weekly meditation session with Nancy. After three months, he was sitting with greater ease and his mind was no longer chasing every thought that floated by.

At that point, Harry realized that Nancy had set an impossible goal, because his mind would continue to have thoughts no matter what. He had learned from mindfulness sitting that the goal was not to stop having thoughts, but to let thoughts flow by without any judgment. He let Nancy know that he felt their bet was rigged, and she laughed. "Yes, you are learning!

You can win our bet if you can sit without following or judging any thoughts in your thirty-minute sitting."

Harry won the bet after six months, and instead of insisting that Nancy take him to dinner, he thanked her for pushing him into sitting, and took her out instead.

Interestingly, Harry began extending his mindfulness to caring about others. He realized that he did not have to be "number one" and defeat others in order to achieve his academic and career goals, because he could achieve his aspirations by doing his best. He could enjoy his studies, and his friends, and still be successful.

An important part of being compassionate to ourselves is to stop self-criticism, which is unproductive. In Buddhism, we learn to let go of our regrets about the past, and accept our bodies and our personalities without judgment. When we have a negative reaction, such as getting angry at our partner and shouting unkind comments, we take a break to become in touch with our love and compassion for this person. Visually, we can stamp out the demon of anger, which is a *klesha*, or mental poison. We can apologize to our partner for our angry words and then let all memory of the event fade away.

The Dalai Lama teaches that empathy leads to becoming more compassionate in our connections to others. He suggests putting ourselves in the other person's place to understand how we would react in their situation.

TOO MANY CHOICES

When my Buddhist friends and I talk about which *klesha*s dominate our thinking, greed and anxiety leap up. We find it hard to put aside materialistic desires as we go about our daily activities, because everywhere we go, we find the media telling us about new ways to make our lives healthier or more fun, and run into friends telling us about something they just bought that we suddenly feel we have to get for ourselves or our kids.

Anxiety also keeps nagging us, as our work demands and family needs keep us glued to our to-do list. Our minds keep up an endless chatter, so we are lost in our thoughts instead of enjoying the moment. Although we may be lucky in our lives, with good jobs and wonderful children and friends, we are stressed out and don't have time to enjoy life. We are tired, we are overwhelmed, and we are frustrated. Our inner wealth supposedly is inexhaustible, but we feel exhausted by life.

Working parents especially are overwhelmed trying to balance work and family demands, and many working parents feel they spend too little time with their kids, and even their partners. Working moms and dads report feeling tired and rushed, and it affects how much they enjoy caring for their children. Working parents want more leisure time to spend with friends or on outside interests. Level of education doesn't seem to make a difference in finding a balance. In fact, college-educated parents find it even harder to balance work and family. One source of our feeling rushed and overwhelmed is society's endless list of what "good parents" do for their children: enroll them in sports or ballet or drama, fix healthy meals, supervise school work and computer time, buy the latest fashion fad, and the list goes on and on. Finding balance in life involves managing our goals and expectations as we figure out how to live life.

A visible sign that our life is out of kilter is the clutter that fills our homes. We continuously plow through the mess and keep adding to the piles. Instead of feeling happy with all our belongings, we feel overwhelmed. Popular books tell us how to get rid of unused stuff in our closets and drawers, promising that tidying up will make us happier and bring us a sense of joy.

Our clutter is a symbol of what is wrong with our lives in a materialistic, affluent society that provides too many choices. We face an incredible number of choices in every aspect of life: endless displays of jam and cereal at the supermarket, rows of products at the consumer electronics store, cell phone apps for every whim, health care options foisted upon us in both sickness and health, and a multitude of colleges that all provide an outstanding education. Economic theory tells us that maximizing choice maximizes freedom. Instead of making us feel freer or happier, though, too many choices can frustrate and paralyze us. We end up less satisfied once we finally make a choice, because we have regrets about the choices we gave up. So much choice also results in an escalation of expectations. Then we blame ourselves if our experience is disappointing.

My students often remark in their journals about becoming overwhelmed when they take a trip to the supermarket. One student wrote, "There are (and I'm not exaggerating) at least 30 different brands of butter. So I found myself thinking, who would ever need this many choices for butter??? Sure, you have low fat butter and unsalted butter and spreadable butter, but I'm talking at least 30 brands that each carried every type of butter your heart could desire. We had no idea what butter to pick, completely derailed by this abundance of such a basic good." Their experiences give me a jolt because I have learned to minimize my grocery shopping time by always buying the exact same brand. Like most of us, I don't bother to keep up with all the "new" choices, and didn't even know there are so many choices for butter.

My approach to grocery shopping is an example of the economic solution known as "satisficing," or making an acceptable decision based on incomplete information. We end up with something that meets our needs without taking an excessive amount of time or energy to make the "best" decision.

But satisficing doesn't address the problem faced by many people who have too few choices because they are too poor to purchase essential goods. The poor endure lives of desperation as they struggle to buy basic shelter, food, health care, and transportation, and try to have at least some money left over for family and community activities. Vacations are not part of their lives. The poor struggle to manage with less than they need, which results in their becoming preoccupied with scarcity and paying little attention to other things. The vicious cycle of poverty rules their lives: they can afford to live only in neighborhoods with bad schools and crime, and their children get an inadequate education so they end up with lousy jobs, or no jobs, and can only afford to live in bad neighborhoods with bad schools. The poor lack access to good food and nutrition, and their health suffers, as they experience higher rates of obesity, diabetes, asthma, and death at a younger age.

In stark contrast, we see the trappings of the rich all around us. Rich celebrities and executives design their "dream homes"—overt paeans to wealth and power with dozens of bedrooms and bathrooms built with exotic materials, lavish displays of art and furnishings, and multiple closets for storing clothes and an endless stream of expensive purchases. Their sprawling homes have no close neighbors, and they are surrounded by fences and security systems so that they do not have to interact with the public. Often, the rich also have their superyachts, and when not traveling by superyacht, they travel by private jets as they drive up the demand for extravagant vacation spots around the globe.

We can improve people's lives in both affluent industrial societies that have too much choice and in poorer countries that have too little choice by redistributing income from affluent to poor countries so that we have less choice and they have more. Then rich societies will consume fewer fancy foods (or houses or cars), and poor societies have more basic food (or shelter or transportation). In a Buddhist economy, everyone will be better off.

INCOME AND HAPPINESS

In general, when their income is adequate, people use their resources and talent in such a way that they feel satisfied with life. But does their happiness increase with higher income?

You might expect it to do so, but comparisons of income and happiness across developed countries find that national happiness does not increase with national income. This observation is known as the Easterlin Paradox: once basic needs are met, as average per capita national income grows, average national happiness tends to remain the same over time.

Psychologists explain this by pointing to people's adaptability to situations or events, both good and bad. People fear bad events, but fortunately, we are not as affected by bad events as we expect to be. This is also true of good events. In addition, people strongly prefer avoiding a loss to acquiring a gain, which

economists call *loss aversion*. Although we may eagerly antici-
pate or enjoy a good event or outcome (receiving a promotion,
winning a game, buying a new car), we soon adapt to it and
return to our baseline sense of well-being.

What do we observe in rich countries when we compare
income with *quality of life*, which is measured by physical
and mental health, educational attainment, drug use, and
obesity? We find that these quality of life indicators are
not related to average national income, and that they
worsen as income inequality rises across countries. Let us
emphasize this important outcome: *Happiness and quality of
life are related to a country's level of income inequality, but not to its
average income.*

Unfortunately, this pattern has held true in the United
States, where indicators of health and well-being have fallen as
income inequality has increased relative to other affluent countries. Today, U.S. indicators of mortality, life expectancy,
childhood poverty, incarceration, and general health put the
United States at or near the bottom among high-income countries, although as recently as 1980, when income inequality was
not so stark, the United States was closer to the top. Another
study shows that the U.S. disadvantage in postneonatal
mortality compared to Europe is driven almost exclusively by
excessive inequality.

Although national happiness does not improve with national
income, if we look *within* a rich country, the quality of life indicators do improve with income, so that a family's health, educational attainment, and other quality of life measures increase as
income increases. Also within a country, life satisfaction or
happiness increases as you move up the relative income scale.

This supports the relative income theory, which holds that a family's well-being and life satisfaction depend on its income relative to other families. As national inequality increases, the difference in income between those at the top and the other 99 percent widens, and the typical family's well-being declines. Once again, we see that average national income does not tell us much about how well an economy is performing in terms of creating well-being for all people.

Acknowledging our interdependence with others shows us the injustice of income inequality. Rising inequality harms us all as the health and social problems of those at the bottom worsen. Throughout history, philosophers have argued against extreme gaps in income and letting some people live in dire need. In ancient times, Plato thought that both poverty and extreme wealth have negative consequences for individuals and society. In modern times, the philosopher John Rawls argues that social and economic inequalities are just only if they provide compensating benefits, especially for the least advantaged members of society, and if every person possesses the primary or basic goods required to function in the society. When surveyed, Americans agree that inequality is harmful and think that government policies can, and should, reduce the gap between the rich and everyone else.

Free market economists assume that inequality is required in order to provide incentives for people to work hard and be rewarded for their contributions to the economy. But does inequality actually provide incentives by rewarding good performance? A recent study of CEO pay (value of total annual compensation) and the performance of the CEO's company shows that as CEO pay goes up, the company performance goes down. CEOs with lower pay run companies with better performance. Furthermore, the negative relationship between CEO pay and company performance was most pronounced in the 150 firms with the highest-paid CEOs. Yet we don't hear economists advocating policies to reduce CEO pay in order to improve company performance, and free market economists continue to argue that outrageous CEO pay provides required incentives.

MATERIAL WELL-BEING

The distribution of income across families is critical to evaluating a country's well-being and how people actually live. Families' evaluation of their quality of life reflects their relative income as well as their total expenditures, because a family judges its standard of living by what the income groups above it are consuming. You can see how an increase in income inequality results in people trying to increase their consumption in order to maintain their relative consumption and keep up with the higher-income groups. With more inequality, a society becomes less satisfied with the same national income.

Economists have traditionally divided family consumption into three categories: basics (necessities), variety (comforts), and status (luxuries or positional goods). Basics are the goods and services that most families consume, and include expenditures made to meet fundamental physical needs, such as food and shelter, and minimum requirements to function in society, such as transportation and recreation. Expenditures above the basic requirements can be broken down into variety, which makes life more comfortable and interesting, and luxuries, which provide status markings of social position through showiness or exclusion. The same expenditure can include basics, variety, and status. For example, the amount a family pays for shelter includes the minimal amount required to rent an adequate place (basics), plus the additional amount to pay for enough rooms to be comfortable (variety), plus the additional amount for the mansion in a swanky area with a large lot and fancy gates to mark position and provide privacy (status). Families can play at the local playground for basic recreation, or drive to a nearby state park for a weekend trip for more variety, or spend tens of thousands of dollar for an exclusive, luxurious hideaway separated from the masses on a cruise ship.

With economic and technological development, the basics expand and change. Variations in basics across countries reflect both culture and level of economic development. Although the ability to purchase basics may be viewed as critical in defining a family's well-being, the family may be observed purchasing variety or even luxuries in place of some basics because of social norms. An example of this is when a mother spends extra money on a backpack decorated with well-loved characters (variety) rather than the cheaper plain one (basics) so that the child feels like the other kids who admire one another's backpacks.

My own research analyzes how U.S. families from across the earnings distribution spectrum, from laborer to professional, spent their money on basics, variety, and status over the twentieth century. I found that as incomes grew over time, families emulated the spending patterns of higher-income families and also integrated newly available goods and services into their lifestyles. In 1918, wage-earner families were spending 93 percent of their budgets on basics and 2 percent on luxuries. In 1988, they were spending only 55 percent of their budgets on basics, 23 percent on variety, and 22 percent on luxuries. As family incomes increased dramatically over those seventy years, their standard of living improved as they consumed more variety. Yet working families felt the sting of rising inequality, as evidenced by their spending on status to emulate families whose incomes were rising even faster.

In Buddhist economics, with reduced inequality and adequate financial security, families no longer yearn for status goods. All families have access to basics, and people use variety to make life more comfortable and interesting. The consumption of status, which marks position, does not add to the overall quality of life because status consumption is based on making one person happier at another person's expense (a zero-sum game); some economists, such as Robert Frank, even call this phenomenon "positional arms races." Buying status is wasteful and does nothing to improve total social welfare.

When inequality increases the income gap between the rich and everyone else, the rich start paying even more for status goods. They buy bigger, more lavish houses to maintain their position relative to other rich people. Then everyone else feels worse off as they fall further behind. Overall, the well-being of the rich hasn't improved with bigger, more luxurious houses, and everyone else is less satisfied with their own houses. One way to stop this spiral of dissatisfaction is for government to impose high luxury taxes on positional goods.

Buddhist economics does not ignore living standards or the material aspects of life. Aesthetics and art are important in Buddhism, because creativity in literature and art, gardening and cooking, has a role in nurturing the human spirit. But attachment to material goods or a certain type of lifestyle is not the driving force in daily life or the national economy in a Buddhist economics world. Instead we use material possessions to engage our talents and develop our human spirit.

WHY DO WE WORK SO HARD?

This question has been asked through the ages, and the prediction that people will quit working so hard and live more balanced lives once their incomes provide a comfortable life is not observed in most affluent societies.

Even so, people in some affluent countries highly value their paid time off to travel (Germany) or to care for their families (Denmark, the Netherlands, and Norway). Although the average workweek is still long (36.8 hours in the Organisation for Economic Co-operation and Development's thirty-four democratic nations), annual work hours in rich countries have gone down as paid vacation time and paid time off for family care have gone up. In Western Europe, paid time off ranges between twenty and thirty days per year. Germans worked an average of only 1,371 hours in 2014, and workers in Denmark, the Netherlands, and Norway worked about 1,430 hours. If these actual hours worked were spread across fifty-two weeks, the average workweek would be only 26 to 27 hours long.

Some rich countries maintain long annual work hours with much less paid time off for vacation and family care. In the United States, annual work hours were 1,789 in 2014, and in Japan, 1,729 hours. The average U.S. worker worked 418 more hours, or about twelve more weeks, than the average German worker in 2014. No wonder we see many more Germans traveling the world than Americans.

Sociologists Helen Lynd and Robert Lynd asked, "Why do they work so hard?" in their classic study *Middletown* in the 1920s. Their answer was, "Both business men and working men seem to be running for dear life in this business of making the money they earn [to] keep pace with the even more rapid growth of their subjective wants."

This sociological answer from almost a century ago mirrors today's economic answer: wanting more money drives us to work long hours. Today we are still running for dear life to satisfy our wants, tethered to electronic devices that allow us to stay connected and work 24/7 from anywhere. Work and leisure hours have merged, work and family and social activities are integrated as we read and send messages and check Facebook and Twitter every few minutes. The idea of shutting the door once we leave work to enjoy our free time has joined the extinction list.

In Buddhist economics, interconnection does not occur on the Internet but in our hearts and in mindful attention to what is happening at the moment. We no longer crave time to enjoy life, because being mindful lets us savor the moment. We can satisfy our consumption needs without overworking, and then we use our talents and resources to help our family, friends, and community, as well as others in distant places who are suffering.

Reducing our own work time is very difficult to do, because workplace norms require long workdays with little time off. If you try to create your own schedule, you can find yourself out the door, or in a cubicle without any prospect of promotion. When people accept a 24/7 work ethic, it is hard to go against the stream without being penalized.

Reducing work hours needs to be done at the national or state level. Developed countries must follow the example of the European countries that have reduced work time, with required vacation time and required paid family leave, as well as retirement early enough to enjoy it. Then more jobs would be available to more people, who could work to their full potential, and we could welcome the automation of work.

Also, everyone needs to feel secure and know that they will not become impoverished because of health problems or job loss. Governments must provide adequate income support policies so that people feel secure and part of society. Shorter work hours, family-focused policies, and income support programs would restore the balance between family and work. Then our economy would be providing the resources and support systems that families need in order to be happy.

REDUCING SUFFERING

Because everyone's well-being is interdependent, reducing suffering is an integral part of the Buddhist economics model and extends into all activities, from the individual to the world.

How to create a just and fair economic system dramatically illuminates how Buddhist economics differs from free market economics. We've already seen that free market economics assumes that markets work well and produce optimal outcomes that maximize social welfare. We've also seen that the competitive requirements that create free markets don't actually exist in the real world. Free markets are a daydream, or a prop in a political debate.

At this point in time, Buddhist economics is also an idealistic daydream, at least in materialistic economies, yet this economic system can be implemented if enough people and governments around the world join together to minimize suffering. By reducing the suffering of people living in dire circumstances without hope, we improve the well-being of everyone. One means of minimizing suffering is to end extreme poverty. In 2010, the United Nations reached its Millennium Goal of halving the 1990 extreme poverty rate. Reaching this goal before the 2015 deadline showed the world that we can, and must, continue to improve the lives of the 1.2 billion people still living in extreme poverty and hunger.

Providing universal health care reduces suffering, and all people should have access to safe, basic surgical care. Yet five billion people, or five out of seven people worldwide, are unable to get lifesaving surgeries, either because a surgical hospital is not nearby or because they cannot pay for the surgery. As a result, millions of people die from appendicitis, childbirth, compound fractures, and other treatable conditions. Providing basic surgical services globally could save 1.5 million lives per year.

Buddhist economics impels us to practice compassion, to care about how each member of society is doing, even if we do not know them, even if they live in another country. Following the models of economists John Rawls and Amartya Sen, we observe whether people have the basic goods considered essential by their communities, and we then evaluate their well-being based upon their capabilities. We care especially about the suffering of families who lack the basics required to be healthy and live comfortable lives.

A Buddhist economic system asks that we relieve the suffering of those who work long hours under unhealthy and painful conditions to make clothes and electronics and an array of other things for us to buy cheaply. Demanding that stores carry only products manufactured under humane conditions, or that food service workers earn a living wage, or that child labor laws be enforced are small steps forward toward this goal. Demanding that our government take action to reduce carbon pollution is another small step. As our daily lives reflect our living more mindfully, we will begin to see many other ways in which we can reduce the suffering of others while our own happiness grows.

Buddhist economics requires a multidimensional evaluation of well-being, which includes assessing the opportunities and capabilities of all people, especially those in extreme poverty. The Buddhist country of Bhutan made headlines around the world when it introduced the idea of using a Gross National Happiness (GNH) Index in place of GDP to measure the nation's prosperity and well-being. The Gross National Happiness Index sets up sufficiency benchmarks, specifying the basics they think everyone should have, in nine important areas of life, including mental and physical health, community vitality, and ecological resilience, and uses attainment of sufficiency in these areas to classify people in four groups, from unhappy to extremely happy. Bhutan uses the GNH to focus on policies that ensure everyone is extensively or deeply happy. (For more on GNH, see Chapter 6.)

WAR AND VIOLENCE

Wars cause an enormous amount of human suffering around the world, yet they are discussed mostly in political terms. The excessive economic costs of war are barely discussed at all.

The U.S. wars against Iraq and Afghanistan have been the most expensive wars in U.S. history, with their combined costs totaling between $4 trillion and $6 trillion, according to research done at Harvard, Columbia, and Brown Universities. The human devastation is mostly ignored, and the American people funded wars that brought about global tragedy, including the destruction of large parts of Iraq, Afghanistan, and surrounding countries and the death of thousands of innocent children and adults as well as soldiers. Yet the human suffering grabs international attention only when it causes problems in other countries, as when millions of desperate Syrian refugees risked their lives to migrate into safer, richer European countries that turned them back.

Obviously, the money spent by the United States has not brought peace to the region. Instead, it has fanned hatred and vows of revenge. Nor have the wars made the United States safer. These trillions of dollars spent on war, which could have been used to provide a higher quality of life for people at home and abroad, have done little more than incite more violence around the globe.

At home the United States also struggles with violence. A lack of gun control laws has brought death to a multitude of innocent people, including children. In 2013, firearms were used in 11,208 homicides (and in almost twice as many suicides), and firearms caused another 33,636 nonfatal injuries. Racism is often part of the violence, and police have been observed beating, even killing, innocent African Americans, many of whom live in fear that their lives are regarded as disposable.

Nonviolence is at the heart of Buddhist economics, which advocates using compassion rather than violence to resolve conflict. Buddhism teaches that one should always avoid being the aggressor, though one can practice self-defense and defend one's own country from attack as a last resort. When addressing the moral issue of entering into war, a country must examine its motivations honestly in order to avoid rationalizing going to war because of fears about another country or religious group, or revenge, or greed. It is all too easy for nations to lie to themselves.

The Dalai Lama tells us, "War and the large military establishments are the greatest sources of violence in the world. Whether their purpose is defensive or offensive, these powerful organizations exist solely to kill human beings . . . I want to make it clear, however, that although I am deeply opposed to war, I am not advocating appeasement. It is often necessary to take a strong stand to counter unjust aggression."

TAKING REFUGE IN COMMUNITY

Buddhism relies upon "the three jewels" to guide and sustain our lives: Buddha, dharma, and sangha. Our Buddha nature nourishes us, the dharma teaches us the path, and the sangha is our community of family and friends, who give us courage and renew our energy. We cannot expect to practice Buddhist economics without a community of like-minded people who share our values and goals.

People need a community for social and emotional support. Family and neighbors, including those who live nearby or share a sport or hobby or religion with us, provide our primary community, which then expands outward to include old friends, people from work, and families we meet through our kids' activities. Within our community, our personal sangha is the group of close friends with whom we share our ups and downs, with whom we feel free to explore our deepest fears and longings. People who love and trust one another, and who put one another's well-being on an equal (or higher) level than their own, become a sangha.

Thich Nhat Hanh teaches us that we amplify our energy to live mindfully and to create change when we join with others. He writes, "Our collective compassion, mindfulness, and concentration nourishes us, but it also can help to reestablish the Earth's equilibrium and restore balance. Together, we can bring about real transformation for ourselves and for the world."

If you do not feel that you have a personal sangha, take the time and care to create one. A sangha is a place where people reach out to help another person who needs compassion and generosity during a difficult time. When we practice kindness to help others without any thought of what they will do for us, then we are building a support network of close friends. Happiness studies show that having people to call on when you need help is an important source of satisfaction in life.

We need to help vulnerable people build social networks that can support them in times of trouble. Communities need to have the capability to work collectively with people and groups, and help them reach out to those in need of supportive social networks. People who are addicted to alcohol or cocaine, for example, must break away from their old pals, who are often addicts as well, and form new supportive communities of friends who do not share their addiction.

Families who can afford to pay for a home in a good neighborhood know the importance of living in a community where people look out for one another and schools provide their children with a good education. Economists know that the neighborhood in which a child grows up has a significant impact on their prospects for the future. Counties can be ranked by their opportunities for a child's upward mobility, which varies dramatically across the states. Look up your county and see if it ranks high or low in providing economic opportunity. Economic studies have found "large differences in individuals' economic, health, and educational outcomes across neighborhoods in the United States."

BECOMING FREE

In Buddhist economics, freedom is achieved when our reality is no longer clouded by concepts and illusions and we see that everything is impermanent and interdependent. No longer is freedom regarded as having the ability to choose from an endless array of goods and services. Now freedom represents many different things, which vary according to a person's values and goals and a country's culture and politics.

In the developing world, of course, human rights, especially for women and children, are critical in determining if people are free. Buddhist economics is based on the principle that everyone should have the capabilities they need to live meaningful lives, and central to having those capabilities are human rights, with a transparent and honest government.

In rich democratic countries, where human rights are widespread and protected by law (although racial and sexual discrimination and violence still exist), freedom usually means having the right to say and do and live as one pleases, without interference from other people or the government. But in Buddhist economics, freedom goes beyond that: Freedom is having the capability to live a fully developed and meaningful life, free from the suffering that comes with *klesha*s, or harmful thoughts and actions, and being interdependent with others and the earth.

In Buddhist economics, taking care of our human spirit is part of our lifestyle. Once we replace maximizing our own income and status with being connected to and caring about others; once we let go of desire and attachment and focus on how fortunate we are; once we surrender our ego with its incessant demands, then we realize the beauty and joy in our lives.

Chapter 4

INTERDEPENDENT WITH OUR ENVIRONMENT

> *You care for each other and many creatures,*
> *As humans gaze at your magnificent glory.*
> *For centuries, you courageously stand tall through*
> *storms, and fires, and drought.*
> *You ask for nothing, until now.*
> *You reach out to humans,*
> *Beg them to stop their violence to Nature,*
> *To go beyond the carbon economy, to stop war.*
> *May we listen*
> *And learn.*
>
> —Forest Nymph, "Ode to the
> Redwoods" (August 2015)

O̤ur fossil-fuel-based economic system is killing Mother Earth and in particular threatening human existence. Human activities have been spewing carbon dioxide into the air, destroying forests, and fouling water since the Industrial Revolution began over two centuries ago. The earth as we know it cannot survive this onslaught. We must end our dependence on fossil fuels and our wanton misuse of natural capital and learn how to live as part of our ecosystem, with sustainable use of energy, land, and water. Climate change is already harming, even killing, humans and other species with extreme storms and drought, rising sea levels, and dwindling water supplies. These problems will accelerate as the CO_2 already in the atmosphere continues to warm the earth for decades to come. If people and nations do not act quickly to heal our ecosystem, future generations may not be able to live on Earth.

Recognizing that humans are part of the ecosystem, Buddhist economics connects our daily activities to the environment, and we naturally care for the earth in our daily lives. No longer do we regard our environment as something to be exploited for profit or personal gain. Buddhist economics has us focus on reality and on our interdependence with nature and one another, so that we can see the worth and beauty of each person, each species, each plant. Instead of exploiting and controlling, people use their knowledge, will, talents, and freedom to live well, in a way that nurtures Nature.

By measuring how our actions affect the environment, Buddhist economics supports the goal of *doing no harm*. Sustainability is an explicit part of the Buddhist economics model, with the requirement that all people must be involved with caring for and healing our planet and stopping its relentless destruction. Using our knowledge, experience, and talents, each of us has something to offer. Together we can create new ways of living on our planet that benefit all.

Experience has taught us that more knowledge or information does not necessarily lead to behavioral change or political action. People can accept that damaging anthropogenic climate change exists and yet not change their lifestyles in any way. People can also reject climate science on the basis of their individualistic ideology or right to consume as they wish.

PUBLIC RESPONSE

Although climate change is a reality, it can be difficult to understand and to act upon. Climate change involves a complex science that is hard for nonscientists to grasp, but we must understand it if we are to develop and advocate economic policies aimed at mitigating the disaster that has already begun. Moral reasoning about the environment provides direction, but alone it does not translate into direct and quick action. People and companies also respond to economic incentives, and nations must use prices and regulations to build a sustainable economy.

Scientists have shown that the sixth extinction, as the ongoing extinction of species is known, is already well under way. Their research has provided us with the knowledge of the required reductions in greenhouse gas (GHG) emissions the world needs to make. Ecological economists have suggested ways in which the global economy can function sustainably within the ecosystem, and a moral imperative to stop global warming has been laid out by our religious leaders. Politically, the world moved forward in December 2015 when 195 countries adopted the first universal climate agreement to limit global warming to 2°C at the UN Climate Change Conference in Paris (COP21). Leaders from 175 countries met at the United Nations on Earth Day, April 22, 2016, to sign the agreement. Now we must push countries to follow through on their promises because in many countries, including the biggest polluters, China and the United States, politics stands in the way of implementing policies to meet the 2°C target.

We have the knowledge required to heal the planet, and a moral imperative to do so. Now we must find the will to take action, both as individuals and as nations, to heal ourselves and the earth. The public response to climate change must integrate four forces: *scientific*, *economic*, *moral*, and *political*.

The Science

Our fossil-fuel-based economy has already destabilized several critical planetary ecosystems. Numerous studies from scientists around the world document the environmental degradation that has occurred and how global warming will continue to harm our lives in the decades to come. In 1988 the United Nations created the Intergovernmental Panel on Climate Change (IPCC) to bring together hundreds of scientists from around the world to study the causes, impact, and mitigation of climate change. The IPCC's Fifth Assessment Report (2014) decisively pointed to human activities as the primary cause of rising GHG emissions that are causing global warming and changes in our ecosystem. Unless countries immediately reduce these emissions, especially CO_2 in industrialized countries and particulate emissions in developing countries, humans will have to live with more violent and unpredictable storms, severe flooding, horrendous droughts, diminishing agricultural output, and rising sea levels.

For over three decades, the early warnings of climate change by expert Jim Hansen and activist Bill McKibben fell on deaf ears. Hansen's testimony to Congress in 1988 explained global warming and called for action to reduce carbon emissions. McKibben's 1989 book, *The End of Nature*, dramatically portrayed the dangers of climate change. Yet most people partied on as if the global warming warnings didn't pertain to them.

SOURCES OF GREENHOUSE GASES AND BLACK CARBON

To stop emitting greenhouse gases, we need to know what they are. Globally, in 2010, carbon dioxide accounted for 76 percent of GHGs (65 percent from burning coal, oil, and natural gas and another 11 percent from deforestation and land use). Methane accounted for 16 percent (from agriculture, landfills, and the production of natural gas, which is methane); and nitrous oxide accounted for 6 percent (from fertilizer use and biomass burning).

The primary economic activities causing GHG emissions are energy generation (mostly of electricity and heat), which accounts for 35 percent, and agriculture (mostly from livestock, rice cultivation, fertilizer use, deforestation, and the burning of fields), which accounts for 25 percent. The amount of GHG from agriculture would be much higher except for the fact the figure subtracts the large amount of carbon dioxide that forest ecosystems *remove* from the atmosphere. Another 21 percent of GHG emissions is caused by industrial production (especially cement), excluding electricity use, plus 14 percent by transportation (cars, trucks, airplanes, trains, and ships) and 6 percent by buildings.

The cement industry deserves special mention, because few people know how polluting it is and because of its importance in economic growth. The cement industry causes 5 percent of global CO_2 emissions, and China produces almost half of the world's cement. Mostly out of sight, concrete is used to make buildings, roads, sidewalks, and dams, and each person around the world "consumes" three tons of new concrete annually.

Global warming is happening because human activity is emitting GHGs much faster than the earth can naturally absorb carbon and radiate heat back into space. Climate scientists measure Earth's energy balance to see whether Earth is gaining energy (as absorbed sunlight) or losing energy (as emitted heat radiation). The energy imbalance reveals the net climate forcings, that is, the imposed additions to the planet's energy balance that increase global temperature. Carbon dioxide in the atmosphere decreases outgoing radiation and causes global temperatures to rise. Nature provides natural carbon absorption, and the main carbon "sinks" are forests, the ocean, and soil. But these natural carbon sinks cannot absorb the amount of atmospheric carbon being emitted by human activity.

In developing economies, there is another major source besides greenhouse gases contributing to global warming: air pollution from black carbon, which consists of fine particles (especially particulate matter, $PM_{2.5}$, or "soot") emitted into the air from the incomplete burning of fuels (primarily plants and trees being burned in the open air and wildfires), people using cow dung and wood for cooking and heating, diesel engines, and industrial production (especially coal power plants and cement-making factories). The World Health Organization estimates that deaths from air pollution totaled 7 million people in 2012, or *one in eight* global deaths. In the poorer Pacific and Southeast Asian countries, 3.3 million people died from indoor air pollution (fumes from cooking and heating), and 2.6 million died from outdoor air pollution (including fumes from cars, diesel trucks, power plants, and industrial factories).

The difficulty of living in badly polluted air is hard to comprehend until you experience it yourself. I learned what this means in daily life when my husband and I arrived in Mumbai in February 2015: immediately, our eyes stung and our lungs screamed to us to slow down because air pollution, or soot, causes permanent damage to your lungs. This degradation affects everyone, including the rich, who cannot shut pollution out of their lives even if they can filter the air in their homes. Then we flew to New Delhi, where the air pollution went from the "unhealthy" level of Mumbai to "hazardous." My husband came down with pneumonia, while I wore a mask to filter out particulates. Odor and smog, along with noisy grid-locked traffic, made walking outside uncomfortable and unhealthy. We left New Delhi with relief, only to find that other cities across north India also had hazardous levels of smog. India has the world's worst air pollution, and New Delhi has the world's dirtiest air.

THE ROLE OF TECHNOLOGY

Even if human activity were to cease emitting greenhouse gases today, and we immediately stopped cutting down the forests that absorb carbon dioxide, global temperature would continue to rise because carbon dioxide stays in the atmosphere for about a century. The earth's natural processes to remove atmospheric carbon and rebalance solar energy is a slow, slow process.

Despite the hopes of many, it's unlikely that new technology, such as geoengineering, which involves large-scale intervention in the earth's ecosystems, can save us. Two major types of geoengineering are currently being studied and developed: carbon dioxide removal, which removes carbon dioxide from the atmosphere to reduce the greenhouse effect and ocean acidification; and solar radiation management, where some of the sun's energy is reflected back into space to counteract the temperature rise. Only time will tell, however, whether either method can deliver on its promises, although many experts argue that we must use geoengineering to keep global warming under the 2°C target because countries will not reduce carbon emissions quickly enough.

A good example of the problems faced in implementing new technology is carbon capture and storage (CCS), which includes carbon dioxide removal at coal power plants. The once-touted method has already cost billions of dollars to develop. But industry has been slow to adopt CCS because of the high costs of both installation and operation. Only one power plant in Canada has installed a CCS system, and that system has underperformed, with lower output and higher pollution and maintenance costs than expected.

Environmentalists are not happy with CCS either, as it involves storing carbon dioxide underground, a potential safety hazard. Scientists also wonder if CCS will have the intended effect of reducing global warming. One study of carbon dioxide removal from the air was extremely disappointing, because it found that CO_2 removal does not have the impact on the oceans that many assumed it would. Even when removing a huge amount of carbon dioxide from the atmosphere each year (five gigatons, or half the CO_2 now emitted annually from human activities), the continual rise in ocean acidity would be barely affected. The problem is that the ocean absorbs carbon emissions and becomes warmer and more acidic with less oxygen. Once we emit CO_2, some of it damages the ocean even if atmospheric CO_2 is later pulled out of the air.

Another consideration to keep in mind is that new technologies tend to have unintended consequences. For example, the development of ethanol turned out to be a bad idea because it uses a great deal of agricultural land and drives up grain prices. Hydraulic fracking, developed with massive government subsidies, seemed to be a good idea at first, too, and it has been successful in making the United States less dependent on foreign petroleum: the United States has become the largest natural gas producer in the world, with U.S. oil production jumping up 80 percent between 2008 and 2014. Unfortunately, large leakages of methane have occurred at the hydraulic gas wellheads and along the pipelines. Fracking also uses an enormous amount of water under pressure, and water sources in surrounding areas often become contaminated. Originally touted as a "clean" fossil fuel alternative for power plants, natural gas with its leakages of methane can cause faster global warming than coal.

Time is short, the costs are high, and there is no silver bullet.

THE OUTLOOK FOR CLIMATE CHANGE

Scientists have been hard at work learning more about the history and impact of global warming, and their new knowledge brings grim news: Climate change is happening even faster than expected, as global temperatures are rising more rapidly than originally predicted. One study shows that 75 percent of today's extreme-heat days and 18 percent of extreme-precipitation days, which are wreaking death and misery around the world, were caused by global warming.

Global warming causes both extreme storms and extreme drought to occur because the warmer atmosphere can hold, and then release, more water. Many places like California depend on snowpack to fill water systems, but warmer weather causes intense rains that may end up flowing into bays and oceans rather than becoming snow in the mountains. This means that there is less ground and surface water for humans to use.

With rising temperatures, the Greenland and Antarctic ice sheets, Arctic sea ice, and glaciers everywhere are melting. As a result, sea levels are rising and threatening coastal cities. The health of oceans also deteriorates as water becomes warmer and more acidic, causing the death of coral reefs and ocean life.

Slow human response to events that happen at a natural or exponential rate is not new. Here is one example from an old Scottish parable. As the story goes, there once was a lake that provided a village with water and fish and a place in which to swim and play. One day, people noticed green algae growing in the lake, but they ignored it because the patches were very small. The next day, a wise woman became anxious and pointed out that the algae seemed to be growing quickly, and the patch had doubled in size overnight. The elders squabbled over what to do. One fisherman argued that they had to take drastic action because the algae would soon cover the lake and kill all the fish. Others disagreed, arguing that they should wait to see if the lake returned to normal; after all, the algae still covered only about 3 percent of the lake. There were lots of opinions, but no action, and it took just five more days for the catastrophe to unfold. The next day, the algae covered one sixteenth (6 percent) of the lake; the day after that, one eighth; and the day after that, one fourth. Dead fish floated everywhere, and the village could not use the water for agriculture and drinking. They began trying to remove the algae from the lake, but it was a lost cause. In one more day, the algae covered half the lake, and on the fifth day, the lake disappeared beneath it.

This exponential (or geometric) growth rate is hard for most people to fathom, but it is not unusual in Nature, when no natural constraints, such as a predator in the food chain, exist. Humans are more comfortable with linear growth, where things grow slowly by a reliable set amount, and they have a hard time believing that calamity can grow so quickly.

In the new millennium, as the public has begun to acknowledge global warming, its impact is reaching dangerous levels. In January 2015, the authoritative journal *Science* published two articles on how quickly human activity is destroying ecosystems. In the first, a team of international scientists reported, "Two core boundaries—climate change and biosphere integrity [loss of biodiversity]—have been identified, each of which has the potential on its own to drive the Earth System into a new state should they be substantially and persistently transgressed." The article concludes that the present goal of limiting global warming to 2°C pushes Earth beyond the climate change boundary. In the second, experts reported that human activity is causing unprecedented damage to the ocean and sea life. Scientists have studied marine defaunation, which is the loss of animals from a marine community, and found that human activities have already damaged and changed all the major marine ecosystems. Rising CO_2 levels have made the oceans

more and more acidic, which has destroyed marine inverte-
brates by dissolving their shells.

FRESHWATER SUPPLIES ARE THREATENED

Glaciers are "retreating" (a euphemism for melting) at an accelerating rate in the Himalayas, Andes, Alps, and Rockies, with
rapid rises in the meltwater pouring out of them, according to a
study based on 5,200 measurements taken since 1850. (You can
view NASA satellite photos and watch the glaciers disappearing by clicking on the red dots at http://climate.nasa.gov
/interactives/global_ice_viewer.) All that meltwater contributes to rising sea levels.

Sixty-nine percent of the fresh water on the planet is held
in glaciers and ice caps, which have held this frozen water
for thousands of years. Groundwater, which is water held in
aquifers (underground layers of rock that are saturated with
water), accounts for another 30 percent of the earth's fresh
water, with the remaining 1 percent found in rivers, lakes, and
the atmosphere. Groundwater supplies are also suffering from
droughts and overuse. Our freshwater supply cannot keep
pace with the large and growing demands of agriculture, which
uses 70 percent of the fresh water being consumed globally,
plus industries, which are mostly in energy-related areas, plus
people. Water management is extremely critical to our future.
Much more water is being withdrawn than consumed, while
much precious fresh water is wasted. A ten-year study of
global groundwater found that water levels in twenty-one of
the thirty-seven largest aquifers, from India and China to the
United States and France, have dropped below their sustainability tipping points, which means that more water is removed

than replaced. The world's most stressed aquifer, the Arabian Aquifer, supplies water to more than 60 million people and is suffering rapid depletion with little or no sign of recharging. Potential water and drought damages are immense. For example, by the end of the century, the United States may face up to $180 billion in economic losses because of drought and water shortages.

The scientific studies of the consequences of global warming and depletion of natural resources keep coming. You can keep up with new findings online. One valuable source is the *Guardian*, a British newspaper that devotes knowledgeable staff to cover climate change: http://www.theguardian.com/us /environment.

THE SIXTH EXTINCTION

To understand how global warming is changing our planet's ecosystems, let us look more closely at the "sixth extinction," which some believe is already under way because of the recent rapid decline of the number of species on earth. Mass extinctions are a rare occurrence in Earth's history. The fifth extinction, when dinosaurs disappeared, occurred about 65 million years ago, and the first mass extinction is dated to 440 million years ago.

How extreme is the modern disruption to biodiversity? One study documents the current rate of extinction of vertebrates (mammals, birds, reptiles, amphibians, and fish) over the past century and finds that it is dramatically high. More species have disappeared over the past one hundred years than disappeared over the previous eight hundred to ten thousand years. Another study estimates that the extinction of species will accelerate as global temperatures rise, with one in six species threatened under current conditions.

For every endangered species, there is at least one "endangering" species, such as humans, whose activities kill species by both destroying habitats and causing global warming. As humans dominate Nature, we become the invasive and endangering species, and we drive out frogs and whales and native plants.

Although climate science is complex, the basic problem is straightforward: human activities spew carbon into the atmosphere, thereby upsetting the planet's energy balance and raising the earth's temperature. When the industrial era began in the mid-eighteenth century, life was transformed. Living standards in industrialized countries rose, and more and more people could enjoy more comfortable and richer lives. Unfortunately, however, the fossil-fuel-based economies also raised the amount of CO_2 in the air from 280 parts per million in 1750 to 400 ppm in 2016.

Even if we are not experiencing the sixth extinction, earth has entered a new epoch, called the Anthropocene epoch, in which human activities shape, and in many cases destroy, the environment.

KEEP IT IN THE GROUND

Climate science provides us with extensive evidence of global warming and warns us that we cannot continue to heat up the earth. The only uncertainties seem to be how much hotter the earth can become without catastrophic outcomes; how quickly the changes are occurring; and how much damage climate change will cause over the coming decades.

The UN's 2015 Paris agreement called for keeping the global temperature rise well below 2°C above preindustrial levels and to pursue limiting the temperature rise to 1.5°C. Although the target of 2°C stretches back to the 1980s, and the European Union adopted the target in 1996, the 2°C target may simultaneously be too difficult for countries to reach and too high for the stability of Earth's ecosystems. To have a 50 percent chance of remaining below the 2°C cap, atmospheric CO_2 must remain under 450 ppm, meaning that cumulative carbon emissions must be limited to 1,100 gigatons between 2011 and 2050. By 2012 the earth had already warmed 0.8°C, and the CO_2 already in the atmosphere will warm the planet another 0.8°C by the end of the century. Even without using any more fossil fuels, the earth will be 1.6°C warmer. The GHG emissions contained in the world's current fossil fuel reserves (oil, gas, coal) are three times higher than the safe target. And the fossil fuel resources that could potentially be exploited in the future are estimated to be over ten times higher than allowed by the safe target. Over 80 percent of current coal reserves, half of gas reserves, and a third of oil reserves must remain in the ground to meet the 2°C target.

Meanwhile, evidence is mounting that this target is too high. Many are now talking about a lower target of 1.5°C warmer, which requires less than 350 ppm CO_2. But the 350 ppm cap is already out of reach. In 2015, Earth's atmosphere reached 400 CO_2 ppm, and we continue to pump greenhouse gas emissions into the air.

You can follow the growth in atmospheric CO_2, and respond with action.

With the devastating impact of global warming already

happening, attention now turns to how the earth will evolve as it becomes warmer and the oceans become more acidic. Humans may have a hard time surviving on most of the planet. Nonhuman life will continue in various forms and shapes, though perhaps not in those that we know and love. New ecosystems will become simpler, with fewer species of animals and plants. Dominant at first will be those species that are able to spread and adapt quickly to new areas and warmer temperatures.

Not long ago, we thought we had plenty of time to transition to renewable energy, develop new technologies, and make our cities more resilient. Now we realize that it is past time to stop using coal, the dirtiest form of energy, and to use cleaner sources of energy for electricity, transportation, and industry. Fossil fuel companies must leave much of the known deposits of gas, oil, and coal reserves in the ground, and should halt additional investments in fossil fuels. We know that we must stop destroying the rain forests, and end the overuse of pesticides, fertilizer, and water in agriculture.

What is keeping us from saving our planet and ourselves?

The Economics

Free market economists argue that if nations and people are not taking the steps required to stop global warming, it means that they think its mitigation costs more than it's worth. In addition, some economists, using cost-benefit analysis, have underestimated the costs of global warming and the benefits of reducing it by focusing on the goals of income growth and maximizing returns on investments in the short run. For example, they compare the returns on investments aimed at mitigating and adapting to climate change to the returns on alternative investments in new technologies, education, and health over a decade. As the arguments go, investments to aid people in poor countries, such as funds for curing AIDS or combating malaria or providing education, have a higher return than investments to mitigate global warming, and therefore these projects should be given priority. Others argue that we must first focus on increasing economic growth in order to reduce unemployment and raise wages, and later deal with climate change. These arguments are myopic because they ignore the imminent and future threats that global warming poses to people living in the developing world.

Buddhist economics, which follows the path of ecological economics, is based on the premise that humans are part of, and interdependent with, Nature. If our generation does not want to pass to our children a world with intolerable temperatures, extreme storms and wildfires, rising sea levels, disappearing food and water supplies, and collapsing ecosystems, then we must apply an economic analysis that interconnects our well-being with the health of our ecosystem.

The free market approach and the Buddhist approach differ in their views of ways to help reduce global warming. In the free market view, markets can be made to work efficiently with the imposition of a carbon tax that reflects pollution costs. Then market prices will result in the correct investments to mitigate global warming. Buddhist economics agrees that a carbon tax would help guide companies and consumers in their energy-related decisions. However, Buddhist economics thinks that markets alone cannot, and should not, control all aspects of how humans use their ecosystems.

SUSTAINABILITY

Climate scientists and market economists have very different answers to the question, "What is sustainability?" Essentially, the question asks whether today's quality of life can be replicated, or even surpassed, by future generations.

Market economics embraces the concept of *weak sustainability*, which means that humans can freely trade off different inputs in the production process. Human-made capital (technology, machines, know-how) and natural capital (forests, minerals, fish) can be used interchangeably in a variety of combinations in production. For example, we can use more technology in place of less energy (or any natural capital), or less technology in place of more energy, without decreasing output. With weak sustainability, natural capital does not constrain production, and humans can control the environment and their use of natural resources. Market models are used to estimate global warming and its economic impact without worrying about destroying critical ecosystems. From the viewpoint of future generations, it does not matter whether the current generation uses up nonrenewable resources or pollutes the atmosphere as long as we pass on enough productive capacity (machines, buildings, technology) and income in compensation.

Buddhist economics, following the lead of climate scientists, takes a *strong sustainability* approach: physical limits on natural capital exist, and critical ecosystems must be preserved. These limitations impose strict constraints on economic activity. Man-made capital and natural capital are *not* the same. Economic analysis of climate change must restrict trade-offs in the production process that recognize the physical limits of natural capital in order to preserve the planet's critical ecosystems.

Strong sustainability views humans as part of Earth's ecosystems; humans should not dominate the environment for their own gain. Cost-benefit analysis based on weak sustainability is no longer useful because trade-offs with natural capital such as clean air and water can no longer ignore natural constraints. When the physical limits of natural capital have been reached, the economy can no longer ignore them. The economic models hit a wall, the wall of natural constraints. We live on a finite planet.

Whether we viewed sustainability as weak or strong didn't make much difference in the past when the global economy was operating way below the critical boundaries for the ecosystems that support life on earth. Trade-offs in production processes could be made without being constrained by natural capital. Scientists have finally succeeded in convincing us that Nature's ecosystems have boundaries, even if the exact thresholds are still unknown.

FUTURE GENERATIONS

Economists have been slow in absorbing climate science and applying it to their simulations, even as the costs of inaction to future generations have become immense. In part, this reflects economists' expertise in making grand simulation models based on weak sustainability. Economists continue to argue about the precise benefits and costs of mitigating global warming, and how quickly to move on reducing carbon emissions.

Their disagreements center on two key issues: how current and future generations value the environment, and how to incorporate the risk of a catastrophic climate outcome into their calculations.

The damage from the carbon in the atmosphere escalates much faster than the amount of carbon emitted annually, because carbon stays in the atmosphere for decades, even centuries. The economic simulations based upon today's energy market prices do a poor job of presenting future costs and benefits of reducing GHG emissions, because the voices of future generations are not heard, while the fossil-fuel energy industry uses its money and power to influence regulations and prices. Market models incorporate today's lopsided distribution of income and power into their cost-benefit analysis, which reproduces inequality both within and across countries and across generations.

An important input in cost-benefit analysis is the value of the ecosystem to future generations, and this is represented by the discount rate (that is, the interest rate) used to compare future dollars to today's dollar. The free market enthusiasts, who assume that future generations will be richer and live well, place a low value on passing on an intact ecosystem and so use a high discount rate. Buddhist economists, who think the well-being of future generations is as important as our own, use a low discount rate.

Many economists agree with the Buddhist economics approach. For example, the Stern Report (2006) to the British government, which analyzed how to avoid imposing extreme outcomes from climate change on future generations, used a low discount rate of 1.4 percent. The report concluded that damages from climate change are large and require immediate reductions of GHG emissions. Other economists take the free market side.

The leading U.S. environmental economist, William Nordhaus, has developed climate change policies based on cost-benefit analysis using a discount rate in the 3 percent to 4 percent range. In 1990, Nordhaus advocated waiting to implement policies to reduce use of fossil fuels, because by his calculations the costs exceeded the benefits.

You might think that it is nitpicking to argue over whether to use a low or a high discount rate, but it makes a big difference when we estimate the costs and benefits of climate change over many decades. Today's valuation of future benefits is much larger with a lower discount rate.

The limitations of the economic forecasting models are known. MIT economist Robert Pindyck criticizes these models because they forecast gradual damage from global warming and ignore possible catastrophic climate outcomes. Climate change models predict a distribution of increases in *average* global temperatures ranging from 0.4°C to 2.2°C by 2050, depending on how much GHG we emit into the atmosphere. Unfortunately, though, the distributions have "long and fat tails," which means that there is a large likelihood of experiencing temperatures above the average. This translates into unacceptable possibilities of calamity, ranging from major reductions in global output to the end of life as we know it. Pindyck recommends using a simple analysis that focuses on a range of catastrophic changes in output (GDP) to provide crude estimations of the net cost of avoiding unacceptable outcomes.

CARBON TAX
One policy that free market and Buddhist economists agree on is a carbon tax, although Buddhist economics does not think

that a carbon tax alone will fix the problem. The price of fossil fuels must include the social cost of carbon, that is, the cost to current and future generations of the pollution caused by a ton of greenhouse gas emissions. Carbon taxes can take other forms, too, such as "cap and trade," which sets a cap on emissions allowed and then companies can buy and sell emissions permits. For a carbon tax to be effective in the global economy, tariffs could be used to enforce compliance among nations.

The carbon tax ensures that pollution and environmental degradation are no longer "free goods." People and firms that use fossil fuels must pay for the pollution and environmental damage they cause. As economists say, the carbon tax gets rid of the "free rider" problem. It raises the market price on fossil fuels, which provides an economic incentive to switch from fossil fuels to renewable sources of energy. Higher fossil fuel prices help companies with low or no carbon emissions to be more competitive, promote investments in clean energy, and give consumers an incentive to use less fossil fuel.

As we experience the damage from global warming and become more aware of the calamity of harming essential ecosystems, our calculations of the social cost of carbon will become more accurate. Now and in the future, we must not let fossil fuel companies intervene in regulating the prices and uses of fossil fuel.

THE FUTURE COSTS OF CLIMATE CHANGE

Climate change threatens the worldview of those who insist that free markets can provide unending material economic progress. Free market advocates therefore fight back and argue that global warming is not happening, or that it is not caused by humans. Their mantra is "full steam ahead" with the world as we know it.

A study by Citigroup and Oxford University demonstrates that "keeping things as they are at any cost" will cost dearly. The study compares the global liabilities, or net costs, of doing nothing to reduce GHG emissions with the costs of undertaking investments to enact a global low-carbon path. The conclusion is that we can afford to act, and we cannot afford not to act. An *Economist* study came to a similar conclusion: by the end of the century, private investors risk losing more than $4 trillion in assets as a result of the devastating effects of climate change, either in the devalued portfolios of fossil fuel companies as fossil fuel use is ended, or in a devaluation across all companies if GHG emissions continue.

The Morality

Pope Francis outlined the moral dimension of climate change in his encyclical letter *Laudato Si*, issued in May 2015. *Laudato Si* begins with an eloquent overview of our relationship to Nature. Pope Francis cries out for the earth, saying,

> We have come to see ourselves as her lords and masters, entitled to plunder her at will. The violence present in our hearts, wounded by sin, is also reflected in the symptoms of sickness evident in the soil, in the water, in the air, and in all forms of life.

The pope then summarizes the basic science of climate change and presents a compelling argument of why activities that cause global warming are immoral. He describes how our economy is based upon a throwaway culture, intensive use of fossil fuels, and deforestation—all of which threaten the planet. He describes the damage inflicted on essential resources such as clean water, agriculture, clean energy, and biodiversity, with the poor bearing much of the burden of the damage. Activities that cause climate change are immoral and a sin because climate change damages the earth and kills people and species, he tells us. We have a moral duty to immediately change our way of living. Collectively we must cease activities that cause global warming, despoil the environment, and overuse natural capital.

Pope Francis argues that all generations are interconnected with one another and with the earth, and that this fact is the basis for mandating that we care for others and for our common home. He observes that Earth's natural capital puts a limit on growth and that a meaningful life encompasses much more than material well-being, which is the same approach taken in Buddhist economics.

However, the pope claims that population growth is not a problem, and here Buddhist economics takes a different path, maintaining that both overpopulation and materialistic life-styles are overtaxing the ecosystem. If we want to provide health care, education, and other basic items of consumption to all people, we must ask, "How many people can our planet sustain?" The human ecological footprint provides the answer, and it is a shocking one: *Our human ecological footprint already exceeds global resources.* Today's human activity is already not sustainable, even though we do not provide basic food, water, shelter, health care, education, and community life to billions living in poverty.

A country's ecological footprint is defined as the amount of land required to support its lifestyle. In 2010, with a global population approaching 7 billion, people used about 50 percent more resources than the planet can regenerate, which translates into an unsustainable ecological footprint of 1.5 Earths. Now imagine that people in developing countries emulate the lifestyle (and median consumption) of people in the United States: suddenly the ecological footprint balloons to a whopping four Earths, and that's without adding in the projected population growth of an additional 2 billion people by 2050.

In Buddhist economics, we can provide adequate food, shelter, and community life to everyone only if we stabilize global population and consume resources more equitably. In addition to the harm that overpopulation causes to the earth, mothers are also harmed when their health is damaged from bearing many children, and families suffer when children don't have enough to eat or don't live to see their first birthday.

The Dalai Lama has been expressing concern about the environment in his teachings for over three decades. His Holiness discusses the fragile ecosystem of the Tibetan plateau and the Himalayan glaciers, called the Third Pole. The Tibetan plateau is 70 percent permafrost, which contains large reserves of carbon dioxide and methane that will be released as the plateau thaws. Temperatures are rising three times faster than the global average at the Third Pole, which contains 40 percent of the world's fresh water and feeds seven major rivers running throughout South Asia. With a smile, the Dalai Lama notes that relying on prayer to God or Buddha seems illogical, because humans created the problem and humans must solve the problem to avert disaster.

Similarly, Vietnamese Buddhist teacher Thich Nhat Hanh, writing in his *Love Letter to the Earth*, focuses on our interdependence with Mother Earth and on the need for us to appreciate and care for her. Earth gave birth to us, and we return to her when we die. Earth provides us with everything we need to live healthy, joyful lives. Thich Nhat Hanh asks us to express our gratitude at each meal, which represents the gifts, such as tea and bread, that Nature has produced.

Buddhist leaders from around the world signed a climate change statement to world leaders in October 2015. They urge the leaders to ensure that the global temperature increase remains below 1.5°C. They call on countries to transition to a low-carbon economy, and on rich countries to provide financing to poorer, more vulnerable ones. The statement also points out that individuals can take actions to "protect our forests, move toward a plant-based diet, reduce consumption, recycle, switch to renewables, fly less, and take public transport."

Other prominent religious leaders also acknowledge the science behind anthropogenic climate change and urge people and nations to work together toward mitigating its causes. Islamic academics came together to write the *Islamic Declaration on Global Climate Change*, which urges the 1.6 billion Muslims worldwide to phase out greenhouse gas emissions and switch to renewable energy sources as quickly as possible. They emphasize that unlimited economic growth in a finite planet is not viable and call for a "fresh model of well-being" that does not deplete resources, degrade the environment, or deepen inequality.

Pope Francis and the Dalai Lama both stress that war is not morally acceptable because of its violence to people and to Nature. Military-related CO_2 emissions are not counted in a

country's emissions statistics. U.S. military operations in the
Iraq War emitted an estimated 160 to 500 million tons of CO_2
between 2003 and 2010, and this doesn't include the direct
emissions from explosions. As health, weather, and security
suffer from climate change, people may become more aware of
it and countries may become more willing to take action. If
not, people and countries will fight over energy, water, and
food, posing a growing threat to the national security of rich
and poor countries alike. This new form of inequality will
strike much deeper at how people live and survive than income
inequality alone ever has. As Secretary of State John Kerry
reminded students in Jakarta in 2014, "climate change can now
be considered the world's most fearsome weapon of mass
destruction."

WHAT YOU EAT AND GREENHOUSE GAS EMISSIONS
Many people are vegetarian because they don't want to have
animals killed for them to eat. But now that we know that
global warming is killing many species, the reason to be vegetarian extends beyond the slaughter of animals for food.

What you eat makes a big difference in the amount of
greenhouse gases emitted. For example, if you eat 100 grams
(3.5 ounces) of meat every day, which is one serving for most
meat eaters, your diet puts out about 7.2 kg of carbon dioxide
emissions. If you are vegetarian, your daily carbon emissions
are half that.

If you are a meat eater, what kind of meat you eat also makes
a big difference. Beef and lamb have a much greater negative
impact on land, water, and carbon emissions than do chicken,
pork, fish, or eggs (Figure 1). If we don't eat beef or lamb, the

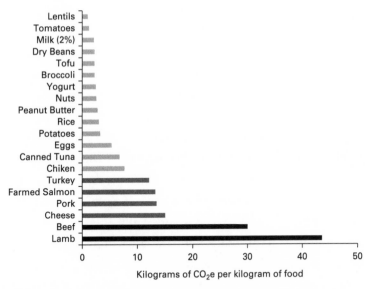

Figure 1: Greenhouse Gas Emissions from Food. Kilograms of CO_2e (carbon dioxide equivalents) per kilogram of food (from farm to table). Source: http://www.ewg.org/meateatersguide/a-meat-eaters-guide-to-climate-change-health-what-you-eat-matters/climate-and-environmental-impacts/. Copyright © Environmental Working Group, www.ewg.org. Reproduced with permission.

environmental damage to the earth from feeding us is greatly reduced, because cattle do not efficiently eat and digest their food, and forests are currently being cleared to raise cattle. Drop beef and lamb from your diet, and then limit your daily consumption of meat to under four ounces. Most likely your waistline will shrink along with your carbon footprint.

While you are cutting your carbon emissions by eating less meat, you will also be using less water. Your carbon footprint and your water footprint walk along the same path. Learn how much water is used to grow certain crops, raise livestock,

and produce other products at http://waterfootprint.org/en
/resources/interactive-tools/.

YOUR ECOLOGICAL FOOTPRINT

When we live in sync with the ecosystem, conserving resources
and caring for the environment has intrinsic value and becomes
a way of life. We sleep our laptop when we take a break, pick up
litter when we go for a walk, buy veggies at the local farmers
market, compost and recycle and put almost nothing in the landfill container, take public transit or bike instead of driving, and
grab a jacket or blanket when we are chilly rather than turning
up the heat. You can add many more ways to be green in your
daily activities. Often these activities are a time for reflection and
appreciating nature as well. For example, taking out the water
recycled from taking a shower or doing the dishes to water plants
outside my door provides a time for me to enjoy the beauty
around me and to connect to Mother Earth, who sustains us all.

In the free market model, a person's time is usually regarded
as being too valuable to waste conserving energy or reducing
waste. "After all," an acquaintance told me, "I make fifty dollars
an hour at work, so I only want to bother with recycling if it's
worth fifty dollars an hour, which it isn't."

In Buddhist economics, we conserve energy and reduce
waste with gratitude. As Thich Nhat Hanh writes, "Caring
about the environment is not an obligation, but a matter of
personal and collective happiness and survival. We will survive
and thrive together with our Mother Earth, or we will not
survive at all."

Take a few minutes to calculate your own carbon or ecological footprint online. You will learn a lot about how you

can make changes to reduce your footprint and live more in tune with Nature. You can calculate your ecological footprint at http://www.wwf.org.au/our_work/people_and_the_environment/human_footprint/footprint_calculator/. You can calculate your carbon footprint at http://www.nature.org/greenliving/carboncalculator/index.htm or http://www3.epa.gov/carbon-footprint-calculator/.

International Action: The Politics

Global warming is hard to tackle because its effects are widespread and don't recognize national boundaries. In contrast, the costs involved in reducing GHG emissions are borne by each country or locale.

No matter how much a nation has caused global warming historically, and no matter how much a nation will suffer from the negative consequences of climate change, we must take actions together on four fronts: (1) mitigate GHG emissions to keep global warming below 2°C; (2) make human communities more resilient to extreme weather and rising oceans; (3) reduce lavish consumption and provide basic consumption to all people; and (4) limit population growth. We cannot trade off among these four goals; each plays a role in creating a sustainable global economy. It is not mitigation versus adaptation, consumption versus population. It is all four.

GHG EMISSIONS NOW AND HISTORICALLY

Because it takes the earth's natural systems decades, even centuries, to absorb atmospheric carbon, the United States and other industrialized countries are responsible for most of the cumulative CO_2 emitted between 1850 and 2007. The United States bears responsibility for 29 percent of the historical carbon dioxide emissions, or as much as the next four countries (China, 9%; Russia, 8%; Germany, 7%; and the UK, 6%) combined. China's economy began growing in the mid-1970s and took off after 2000, and its CO_2 and particulate emissions followed suit.

Let's look at all greenhouse gas emissions, which are mostly from fossil fuels, deforestation, and cement, produced within a country. In 2012, China held the top spot (22.4% of the world's GHG emissions), followed by the United States (12.2%), the European Union 15 (7.0%), India (6.1%), and Russia (4.7%). These top five greenhouse gas emitters were responsible for slightly over half of all the world's GHG emissions.

If we look at CO_2 emissions per person, the United States is rivaled only by Australia among advanced economies. Both countries emitted 17 tons of CO_2 per person in 2010. Other large economies emit much less CO_2 per person: 30 percent less in Russia, 45 percent less in Germany, 55 percent less in the UK, and 70 percent less in China.

Some argue that emissions should be measured by consumption rather than production, because many emerging markets generate CO_2 when they produce goods that are exported and consumed in richer countries. This approach greatly increases the carbon footprint of rich countries (such as Belgium, the United States, Ireland, Finland, and Australia), and lowers it for the developing world (such as China, Brazil, and India). Practically speaking, though, we must measure carbon dioxide in the nation where it is produced, because that is where the government must enforce reductions.

Although the industrialized world is responsible for much of the current global warming from burning fossil fuels in the past, our focus must be on stopping greenhouse gas emissions *today* in order to keep global warming from rising to catastrophic levels. However, instead of leading the way to creating a carbon-free economy, the United States continues to emit large amounts of carbon dioxide. Many Americans seem unwilling to pay for technology that is already available and waiting to be scaled. For example, even with a wide array of energy-efficient vehicles available and government fuel economy requirements on the rise, Americans rushed to buy gas-guzzling SUVs and pickup trucks when gas prices began to fall sharply in 2014. More than half the vehicles sold in 2014 were trucks and SUVs; only 5.6 percent were electric cars and hybrids. Even Americans who care about global warming are not taking the actions required to reduce their carbon footprint.

THE IMPACT OF CLIMATE CHANGE

South Asia and sub-Saharan African nations face extreme risk from the extreme weather, reduced agricultural productivity, and sea level rise caused by climate change. These countries are especially vulnerable because they lack adequate ability to cope with climate impact damages. The online maps at http://www .cgdev.org/page/mapping-impacts-climate-change tell the story.

A recent global study by my colleagues at Berkeley and Stanford, published in the prestigious journal *Nature* in 2015, looked at how temperature affects productivity. Peak economic productivity occurs at an average yearly temperature of 13°C (55°F), and productivity declines sharply as temperature rises. This pattern is observed around the world for both agricultural and nonagricultural activities in both rich and poor countries. The result is that global warming hurts production in tropical countries that already have warm temperatures, and slightly improves productivity in cooler countries as they become warmer. If the world does not reduce global warming, average global production will fall 23 percent, resulting in even more global income inequality because the rich countries are mostly in the cooler climate zones.

The warming of the planet has pushed us past the ability to fully restore the ecosystem. We cannot return to the climate stability of the past ten thousand years because we cannot restore the melted glaciers and ice caps, nor revive the extinct species, nor undo the warmer atmosphere and oceans. The world is at the point where both the mitigation of GHGs and adaptation to damages from climate change are required. In rich countries, economic growth must be based upon investments to mitigate global warming and build infrastructure for adapting to ongoing damage. Development in emerging countries must be built upon clean energy. Buddhist economics teaches us that our economic systems must be decarbonized and renewed with sustainable socioecological practices that go beyond consumption to provide a meaningful life. The new focus is on developing resilient systems that will protect Nature, withstand damages, and rebuild when necessary. The systems must also be flexible and adaptive, and they must incorporate a deep understanding of ecological processes.

COP21 AND BEYOND

I see the 2015 COP21 agreement to "hold the global average temperature well below 2°C above pre-industrial levels"

(Article 2) as acknowledging both the Buddhist economic approach, which follows the United Nation's sustainable development goals, and the free market economic approach demanded by the industrial countries. Countries made *nonbinding* pledges on how they will cut or curb their carbon emissions and protect the forests in order to reach "net zero emissions" between 2050 and 2100. The agreement acknowledges the harm that vulnerable countries face from climate change impacts, but it explicitly excludes providing for any liability or compensation by the rich countries, especially the United States, who are responsible historically for most carbon emissions. Industrialized countries continued their nonbinding goal of aid (current goal is $100 billion) to vulnerable countries until 2025, though the vulnerable countries need even more financial help to transition to renewable energy and develop resiliency.

Even as countries around the world struggle to reach their nonbinding pledges to reduce GHG emissions, we already know that the pledges are not adequate for keeping the global temperature below the 2°C target; global temperature is estimated to increase 2.7°C (or more) even if countries successfully enact their current pledges. COP21 leaders understood that the pledges are inadequate, but they considered them a critical first step toward reducing global warming. To stay under the 2°C target, COP21 set up a review mechanism so that every five years, beginning in 2023, countries can ramp their pledges up over time.

An online user-friendly climate change calculator shows how each country's pledge stacks up. It shows the differentiation required by the emerging countries, which want to continue their economic development for at least the next decade based on fossil fuels, and the industrialized countries, which must immediately begin reducing their GHG emissions.

We hear moans and groans about how much it will cost to transition from fossil fuels to renewable energy, especially from countries and American states that are big producers of coal, oil, and gas. But before you buy into this free market approach, you should know that Stanford University researchers have demonstrated that the conversion to renewable energy provided by wind, water, and solar power (WWS) is technically and economically feasible. Their study provides a detailed roadmap showing how each of 139 countries can transition to renewable WWS energy, with 80 percent conversion by 2030 and 100 percent conversion by 2050. The report provides data on the costs of the conversion, along with estimates of the impact on employment, wages, and health-related costs. Globally, in 2050, the conversion to WWS power, compared to continued use of fossil fuels, saves the average person $170 per year in fuel costs, plus it lowers the average person's damages from air pollution by around $2,880 per year and eliminates another $1,930 per person per year in global warming costs.

The difficulties that countries face in turning their Paris pledges into reality is highlighted by the United States' experience with a pledge to reduce GHG emissions 26 percent from 2005 levels by 2025. This pledge is based upon President Barack Obama's Clean Power Plan, which requires states to reduce carbon pollution from power plants, especially coal plants. The Clean Power Plan was challenged in court, especially by states that mine and generate power with coal. In February 2016, the Supreme Court stayed the Clean Power

Plan, and now its outcome is in limbo. Fortunately, community and state actions, especially on the West Coast and in the Northeast, are making an impact in reducing carbon emissions, but much more still has to be done to fulfill the United States' Paris pledge. If the rest of the world views the United States as abandoning its Paris pledge, major GHG emitters, such as China and India, have an excuse to focus more on economic growth than on reducing carbon emissions.

OUR CARBON-BASED ECONOMIES that have exploited Nature to support consumerist lifestyles have actually ended up having little control over Nature. Instead of trying to dominate the ecosystem to stop global warming, we must realize that we are part of the ecosystem. As Buddhist economics teaches us, survival means adapting to one's environment and caring for it as part of oneself.

We know that moving to a post-carbon world requires the generation of electricity and heat with renewable energy sources, so that industry can use only renewable energy in production and ground transportation can consist only of clean-energy vehicles. Countries must stop deforestation, agriculture must be practiced sustainably, and people must eat less meat. The technology for taking these steps is already available.

We must respond to global warming with a multifaceted approach at all levels—from the personal to the local to the national to the global. Human life as we know it depends on it.

Chapter 5

PROSPERITY FOR BOTH RICH AND POOR

We are resolved to free the human race from the tyranny of poverty and want and to heal and secure our planet. We are determined to take the bold and transformative steps which are urgently needed to shift the world onto a sustainable and resilient path.

—United Nations, *Transforming Our World: The 2030 Agenda for Sustainable Development*

ONCE WE COME to an understanding of the interdependence of all people and base economic performance on the quality of life for all people, then we will be on the right track to push for the Buddhist economics goal of *shared prosperity*—using global resources to provide a comfortable and enjoyable life for people worldwide while living in harmony with our ecosystem. But we are a long way from meeting even the basic requirements of the billions of people who lack adequate food, clean water and sanitation, and shelter. Meanwhile the lifestyles in rich countries have an ecological footprint that will devastate the planet. So how do we create shared prosperity in a sustainable way?

A FRAMEWORK FOR THE GLOBAL SHARING OF
EARTH'S ABUNDANCE

When all people are interconnected, their desires and needs are interdependent. The free market model, in which each person is assumed to have independent and well-defined desires, evaporates. Social welfare is no longer the simple addition of everyone's consumption. Society's well-being becomes much larger than the sum of individual consumption, because your well-being adds to my well-being, and our well-being depends on much more than our income. Well-being ripples outward as we share resources globally.

In free market economics, economic activity pushes forward the creation as well as the fulfillment of desires. Buddhist economics holds that the endless formation of desires causes suffering, and we reduce suffering by making sure everyone has a comfortable life. As an economy becomes developed, the quality of life becomes more dependent on nonmarket activities and on enriching people's lives beyond consumption.

Most people in rich countries can purchase the basics they need for survival, and their quality of life depends both on their consumption of a variety of goods that make life easier and more interesting, and on the condition of their health and social networks. But we have to ask: How much consumption do well-off people need to thrive? We saw in the last chapter that everyone *cannot* enjoy the lifestyles of those living in rich countries, because that would require at least four Earths. Sustainable shared prosperity requires that people in rich countries develop simpler, sustainable lifestyles so that people in poor countries can live comfortably. We must stop creating misery and start sharing prosperity, replace desperation with thriving.

Buddhist economics recognizes the harm that people in rich countries do by buying inexpensive goods made by foreign workers, even children, who work long hours in dangerous conditions at jobs that pay very low wages. This is in marked contrast to free market economics, in which the environment and foreign countries are regarded as resources for rich countries to dominate and exploit. Free market proponents believe that competitive markets ensure the best possible outcome, even if some people are still starving, while aid interferes with global markets and might support corruption. Thus intolerable injustice is tolerated.

GLOBAL INEQUALITY OF WEALTH AND INCOME

The magnitude of global inequality can be hard to fathom unless you have traveled to the slums of Mumbai or rural villages in Ethiopia and seen hungry, stunted children living in dark, crowded rooms or huts without running water or a place to poop. The daily suffering of people who lack basic necessities does not come through in the graphs and tables often used to document poverty and inequality. The data are necessary, however, to understand the magnitude of the problem of how to share prosperity and reduce suffering around the world.

Global wealth is concentrated in the hands of a small group of billionaires, and their wealth has been growing rapidly. The very richest eighty people at the top of the *Forbes* billionaires list own as much wealth as the bottom 50 percent of the population. Imagine—eighty rich people having as much wealth as 3.5 billion people. Many of these wealthy individuals grew rich in a few critical industries, including finance, pharmaceuticals, and fossil fuels, and their companies spent vast sums lobbying for policies to increase and protect their profits and lower their taxes.

Such greed goes beyond comprehension. It is immoral.

We know more about the distribution of global wealth, which is in the hands of a few, than the distribution of global income, which is spread across more than 7 billion people. The good news is that the data we do have show a modest decline in global inequality as the "middle class" grows rapidly in China and moderately in India. The bad news is that inequality of income within most countries has grown, with the richest 1 percent increasing their share of income over the past thirty years. In the United States, income growth has been all but completely captured by the top 1 percent, who enjoyed 95 percent of the country's income growth in the recovery following the Great Recession, while the bottom 90 percent saw their incomes decline from 2009 to 2012.

Let's make the point even stronger about how much income the global rich command: The richest one hundred billionaires in 2012 would still be extremely rich even if they used enough of their $240 billion income to lift the 12.7 percent of the world population out of extreme poverty (less than $1.25 a day).

In Buddhist economics, this vast inequality is unacceptable.

DOES INEQUALITY IN RICH COUNTRIES MATTER?

Although inequality within rich countries appears inconsequential compared to the global income gap between rich and poor nations, inequality still causes unnecessary suffering. People live by the social norms of their communities, and they judge their own economic well-being based on comparisons with others, including people on television and social media. Inequality causes people to feel less well off than they would in a more equitable world. A more equal distribution of income improves social welfare, as invidious comparisons are replaced by communal feelings of belonging and status consumption is replaced by basic consumption.

COUNTRIES CHOOSE THEIR INEQUALITY

Countries vary in how much inequality they tolerate among their citizens, and a country's inequality reflects its national values and culture. Economist Joseph Stiglitz, an expert on inequality, has demonstrated that a country's inequality is not an inherent outcome of capitalism but a choice that the country has made through its national laws and institutions. Some democratic societies, including Sweden, Finland, and Norway, have made child welfare and shared prosperity top priorities, and these countries have achieved widespread income equality, with a high standard of living for all. Other countries have taken an entirely different approach. Stiglitz provides a list of national regulations that have increased inequality in many nations: the proliferation of world trade agreements, the reduction of taxes on income and inheritances, the weakening of labor unions, the meteoric rise of rich financiers following the deregulation of the finance industry, and the increased market power of companies as they consolidate.

A popular measurement, the Gini coefficient, lets us look

quickly at income inequality across countries. The Gini ranges
from 0 (everyone has the same income) to 1 (one person has all
the income). In Figure 2, we can see that Norway and Germany
have much more equality of income, and the United States and
China much more inequality, with India in the middle. Some
people want to dismiss the equality achieved in Norway, Sweden,
and Denmark because they are small countries with people who
look mostly alike. Yet Germany and France, with larger and
more diverse populations, have still achieved much more equality
than has the United States or the United Kingdom. Stiglitz is
right: government policies shape how people share a country's
resources. The goal of shared prosperity is possible.

British economist Anthony Atkinson agrees that equality is a
choice driven by government policies and asks, "What can be

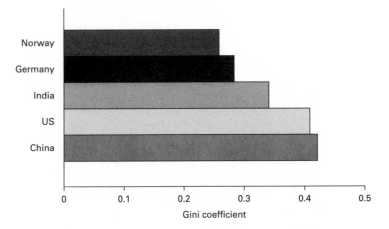

Figure 2: Inequality in Five Countries, 2013. Gini coefficients based on
distribution of disposable income (personal income after taxes and government programs such as Social Security payments). Remember, *lower* Gini is
better (more equal income distribution). Sources: Calculated from OECD
Income Distribution Database (IDD) and UNDP Human Development
Reports.

done?" He takes us on a historical tour to demonstrate how inequality reflects government policies. For example, he shows how a reduction in the tax rates of those with the highest incomes increased the share of income going to the top 1 percent across countries from 1960–1964 to 2005–2009, with the United States and Britain leading the way under the leadership of Ronald Reagan and Margaret Thatcher. To reduce inequality, Atkinson proposes the adoption of fifteen policies, some with proven histories; among them are higher minimum wages, laws that strengthen unions and workers' bargaining power, more progressive income taxes (taxes that increase as income increases) with a top rate of 65 percent, more progressive inheritance taxes, and child benefits. Atkinson then pushes his list further by proposing guaranteed government employment at a living minimum wage for those who cannot find jobs elsewhere, and a capital endowment (minimum inheritance) given to every person when they reach adulthood.

Other economists who care about inequality also back more progressive taxes and other policies that help low-income people. For example, Nobel laureate Thomas Schelling recommends that income taxes automatically increase for top earners when inequality goes up. My colleagues at Berkeley have shown that raising minimum wages in California does not result in reduced employment, because costly turnover goes down as low-wage jobs pay more.

We also observe vast differences in *average* incomes across countries, regardless of how the income is distributed within a country. In 2014, average gross domestic product (GDP) per person was almost $55,000 in the United States, and even higher in Norway, where it was almost $65,000. In the extremely poor

African countries of the Democratic Republic of the Congo and Niger, the average GDP per person was $746 and $938, respectively; and most people lived in extreme poverty, struggling to survive on less than $1.90 per day, or about $700 annually.

GLOBAL EFFORTS CAN REDUCE SUFFERING

The United Nations' push to reduce extreme poverty demonstrates that coordinated effort can pay off. Reduction in global poverty was the major accomplishment of the UN's Millennium Development Goals, a fifteen-year drive to improve the lives of the world's poorest by 2015. The number of people living in extreme poverty fell from almost 2 billion people, an astonishing 43 percent of the population of the developing world in 1990, to just under 900 million people, which was 17 percent of the developing world in 2012. Progress was also made on other Millennium Goals. The child mortality rate declined by half, down to 43 deaths per 1,000 live births, though sixteen thousand children are still dying each day from preventable pneumonia, diarrhea, and malaria, exacerbated by malnutrition. The number of people lacking access to safe drinking water dropped dramatically around the world, from 2.6 billion in 1990 to 663 million people in 2012, but access to sanitation facilities lags far behind; one in three people (2.4 billion) is still without adequate sanitation facilities. Enrollment in primary education has risen to 91 percent, and women's positions have improved, with more employment available to women outside agriculture and more women in elected national positions.

In 2015 the UN adopted the even more ambitious Sustainable

Development Goals (SDG) to take us through to 2030. The new plan is complex, with 17 interrelated sustainable development goals and 169 targets. This chapter on shared prosperity draws specifically on three of them: reducing inequality (goal 10), growth (goal 8), and sustainable consumption and production (goal 12).

Don't let the seventeen goals make your eyes glaze over, because the Sustainable Development Goals can be summarized in the Five P's, which echo Buddhist economics:

People: ensure that all human beings can fulfill their potential in dignity and equality and in a healthy environment.

Planet: sustainably manage natural resources and take urgent action on climate change so that the planet can support the needs of the present and of future generations.

Prosperity: ensure that all human beings can enjoy prosperous and fulfilling lives and that economic, social, and technological progress occurs in harmony with Nature.

Peace: foster peaceful, just, and inclusive societies that are free from fear and violence.

Partnership: mobilize all countries and the means to achieve these goals, especially those focused on the needs of the poorest and most vulnerable.

On the negative side, the UN development goals—both old and new—have been stymied by the global recession that began in 2008, wars in the Middle East and Africa, and political instability. On the positive side, though, much has been achieved. In addition to reducing the number of people living in poverty worldwide, the UN's efforts have led to a sharp reduction in the number of cases of malaria worldwide. The rich world has provided a tenfold increase in the international financing of malaria prevention and treatment programs since 2000, and more than 6.2 million deaths from malaria have thus far been prevented. The global malaria incidence rate has fallen by over a third, and the mortality rate has fallen by more than half.

What this indicates is that when the rich world decides to take action and provide resources, positive results can happen quickly. Extreme poverty and preventable disease in a world of plenty are immoral, and the rich world can and should end both without delay. We can accomplish the goal of all people living comfortable lives with dignity in a sustainable world that respects human rights.

Although resources provided by rich countries to poor countries is an important part of relieving suffering in Buddhist economics, some experts argue that the transfer of money can fall prey to human greed and not lead to the development of programs that improve people's lives. In countries that lack adequate structures of governance, with corruption siphoning off resources, foreign transfers become problematic. Even many pro-equity economists argue against aid because of the corruption. For example, New York University's economics professor William Easterly argues that providing aid to poor countries is not effective because their top-down technocratic approach does not improve individual rights and freedom, and it supports corruption rather than local programs. Others, such as the UN Secretary General Ban Ki-moon and the sustainable development economist Jeffrey Sachs, push rich countries to commit 0.7 percent of their GDP as official aid to the developing world, because they view aid as an essential tool to relieve suffering in poor countries and to help those countries develop sustainable economies.

The rich countries' aid supported the UN's Millennium Development Goals, and while the end results were positive, both the results and the amount of aid fell short of expectations. Too much of the aid was used for the foreign policy goals or commercial interests of the donor countries. More than half of the aid went for debt relief, especially to banks in order to avoid bankruptcies. Much of the remainder was diverted to military aid or natural disaster relief.

Buddhist economics would stop aid that is based on the donor country's own interests, and that often lines the pockets of greedy leaders. The right kinds of aid for projects that promote health and well-being, especially for the poor, and that are financed at the higher amounts previously promised but not yet delivered could save millions of lives each year and end extreme poverty.

ENTER THE GLOBAL WARMING CRISIS

Extreme weather and natural disasters caused by climate change have put pressure on food and energy prices and resulted in death and disease in poor countries, where damage from climate change threatens to wipe out the past half century of improvements in economic development and public health. People in poor countries emit almost no CO_2, but they bear much of the brunt of the damage from global warming. The poor are the least able to endure the deteriorating quality of life with their very survival threatened by diminished food supplies and physical dislocation, along with health problems that result from the increased heat, floods, drought, and intense storms.

Meanwhile, rich nations continue to prosper from industrialization built on fossil fuels whose CO_2 emissions will continue to heat the planet for many decades. The bottom line: poor countries are helping to pay for rich countries' continuing economic growth.

Complicating the matter further is the fact that emerging countries now want their turn at economic growth built on cheap energy. The growing use of fossil fuels in China, India, Russia, Brazil, and Indonesia is causing enormous GHG emissions (discussed in Chapter 4).

We must ask the contentious question, "What is the obligation of the industrialized countries to help the developing countries?" Buddhist economics thinks it is time for rich countries to share prosperity with poor countries, but rich countries don't want to shoulder much of the burden. At the UN Climate Change Conference in Paris (COP21), rich countries were not willing to assume liability for climate change damages, and agreed to provide only a somewhat miserly $100 billion annually to aid poor countries in their transition to clean energy. China alone invested more than this in renewable energy in 2015.

The rich countries, led by the United States, remain greedy in their use of global resources and continue to harm the ecosystem while using their high GDPs to respond to natural disasters, invest in renewable energy, and create more resilient cities. Here are the shocking numbers: The United States has 4.4 percent of the world's population, produces 24 percent of global GDP, and is responsible for 15 percent of global CO_2 emissions. The European Union represents 7 percent of world population, 22 percent of world GDP, and 11 percent of global CO_2 emissions. Disparities among countries are large even within the EU, with 7 of the 28 EU countries accounting for 77 percent of the total EU emissions. Here is a simple summary of carbon inequality: the poorest half of the world's population contribute only 10 percent of global carbon emissions, while the richest 10 percent produce half of the emissions.

Rich countries cannot demand that the developing world, led by China and India, forgo emulating the West's standard of living as their economies grow. Instead, rich countries must lead the way in reducing the environmental damage caused by their profligate use of energy and natural resources, and must work with countries around the world to achieve sustainable economic growth that provides comfortable living standards.

ECONOMIC GROWTH TO THE RESCUE?

We have already wasted the opportunity to use the economic growth of the past three decades to invest in renewable energy sources and reduce greenhouse gas emissions. Now rich countries must decouple economic growth from ecological damage by using their vast resources to switch to clean energy, build modern transportation systems, use agricultural methods that don't involve pesticides and overwatering, create energy-efficient buildings and homes, build sustainable water systems, end overconsumption, eliminate waste, and regulate industrial practices to end exploitation of natural resources and improve working conditions. Fortunately, with even small efforts by governments and companies to be more energy efficient and use more renewable energy, GHG emissions are slowly becoming decoupled from GDP growth in many countries. However, rich countries have yet to change their mindset of "more is better." Their economic growth imperative continues to focus on ever-increasing consumption rather than basing economic growth on building a sustainable world.

The sustainable development expert Jeffrey Sachs explores how the rise of free market ideology and the decline in the role of government in the United States that began in the 1980s led to excess consumption and obsessive pursuit of wealth. His book *The Price of Civilization* argues that the decline in civic virtue, especially among the rich and powerful elite, led to the U.S. economic crisis of 2008 and beyond. Sachs lays out the path to renewed prosperity: "To resist the excesses of consumerism and the obsessive pursuit of wealth is hard work . . . We can escape our current economic illusions by creating a mindful society, one that promotes the personal virtues of self-awareness and moderation, and the civic virtues of compassion for others." Buddhist economics echoes this pathway to national prosperity and happiness.

As long as a sizable number of people in rich countries maintain their extravagant and wasteful lifestyles with gas-guzzling cars, energy-guzzling houses with barely used rooms, wasted food, and landfills overflowing with discarded things, we have no hope of saving our planet. People in the developing world want the same lifestyle we have in the rich countries, and so they imitate our extravagant, wasteful ways. But shared prosperity requires that the top 60 percent or so of people in rich countries simplify their lives, and that all of us live more mindfully—this is the heart of Buddhist economics.

I saw the dilemma clearly when I landed in Colombo, Sri Lanka, in February 2016. The streets were gridlocked with large, expensive imported cars (BMWs, Audis, Mercedes Benzes), and the wealthier neighborhoods were filled with large houses with large gardens. The professional and business class in Sri Lanka, as in other developing countries, are adopting a Western lifestyle as their incomes grow, causing air pollution, inadequate water supplies, and overflowing landfills, not to mention a foreign trade imbalance with imports of foreign cars and petroleum.

Meanwhile, the bottom 80 percent of Sri Lanka's population lives in dire need of basic goods. Sustainable development in their world would mean providing *everyone* with access to healthy food, secure housing with flushing toilets, running water, a kitchen with a stove (powered by renewable energy), good electric trains (also sustainably powered), public education, health care, connection to the Internet, and respect for all religions and for human rights. Developing countries can leapfrog over old technology based on fossil fuel and use modern "green" technology to provide energy, communications, transportation, and sanitation. People's health and capabilities would improve along with the country's trade balance, which would no longer be dominated by importing petroleum products.

The bottom line is that for sustainable development to be implemented in Sri Lanka and worldwide, the rich everywhere, which includes most people in rich countries, must simplify their lives and reduce their ecological footprint.

The United Nations implicitly recognizes this with their sustainable consumption and production (SCP) goal. SCP is viewed as "doing more with less": reducing resource use, waste, and pollution in both production and consumption while increasing net welfare and reducing poverty worldwide.

Each of us should practice sustainable consumption and figure out how to reduce our own personal carbon and ecological footprints. No longer can ignorance and inertia be excuses for adding to global warming and living a lifestyle that is not sustainable. Buddhist economics has shown us the policies needed to create a sustainable, equitable economy. We must demand that our governments adopt these policies, and adapt our own lives to meet these goals.

In the meantime, we can learn from two global crises that are causing unnecessary human suffering: the weak Greek economy and the Syrian refugee crisis. Policies based on Buddhist economics, rather than on free market economics, would be a better approach to both these crises.

End Austerity as a Global Policy

The world has a glut of savings to invest, but little of it ends up in the developing world, where productive investments could build infrastructure and livable cities in a sustainable economy and provide a good return. As Joseph Stiglitz tells us, "the world's financial markets, meant to intermediate efficiently between savings and investment opportunities, instead misallocate capital and create risk . . . [Western financial institutions] are wizards at market manipulation and other deceptive practices."

Ever since John Maynard Keynes, whose theories explained the relationship between government budgets and national output, many economists—including Nobel laureates Stiglitz and Paul Krugman today—believe that austerity in the midst of a deep recession only lowers national output and increases unemployment. Forced austerity drives national economies into a downward spiral; to demand that debt-ridden countries ensure repayment of debts to the International Monetary Fund (IMF) and to private banks is to focus on the health of the financial community at the expense of the lives of people and the health of nations. We have seen this practice play out again and again in countries in South America and Asia, and yet

political and financial leaders never learn that austerity does not
help but actually hurts a depressed economy.

Today, the austerity nightmare is being repeated in Greece as
the European Troika (the European Commission, European
Central Bank, and IMF) refused to restructure the Greek debt
to make it manageable. Austerity actions undertaken by Greece
caused its real economic output to fall more than 20 percent
between 2009 and 2013, and youth unemployment jumped to
60 percent (from a low of 20 percent). As wages and incomes
fell, poverty increased, and the Greeks tried to rebel. Well-
known economists publicly supported them, calling for an end
to the Troika's austerity demands and advocating instead a
focus on refinancing debt, growing the economy with investments and spending, and reducing tax evasion and corruption.
But rebelling against the global financial sector resulted in
Greece's defaulting on its IMF loans, which then forced a
restructuring of the debt and more austerity policies. The
Greek economic crisis continues.

Following the path of the Keynesian economists, Buddhist
economics advocates policies that restructure debt burdens to
manageable levels, that use government spending to restore full
employment, and that reduce greed and corruption. Austerity
based on free market economics results in needless suffering by
millions of people, with the fruits of the economy going to rich
creditors. We know how to do better.

Caring for Refugees Displaced by War

Civil wars and multinational invasions have devastated large
regions, especially in the Middle East, in recent decades.

Displaced from their homes and villages, families have fled to refugee camps, which often cannot provide the food, water, shelter, sanitation, and protection required for survival. Facing death in squalid conditions, families often leave the camps in search of safe places to live.

The current Syrian civil war has created a humanitarian and refugee crisis of horrific proportions, with almost 5 million Syrians taking refuge in other countries and another 6.5 million people displaced inside Syria itself. Over half the refugees are children, often separated from their families.

Most of the Syrian refugees have fled to Turkey, Lebanon, and Jordan, which do not have adequate resources to care for such a gigantic influx of people. The United Nations is urging other countries to step up and take in some of the refugees and fund their resettlement. The Germans, under the leadership of Chancellor Angela Merkel, have tried to draw up a plan with other European countries to take in refugees, but the overall European response has been, "Do not come to Europe." And the response of the United States, which has accepted only fifteen hundred Syrian refugees since 2011, has been equally appalling; in November 2015, the governors of thirty-one states protested the admission of refugees into their states. The result has been chaos across national borders and on the sea as refugee families desperately try to find a safe haven.

The billionaire financier and philanthropist George Soros has put forth a straightforward plan for accepting and caring for the Syrian refugees. His plan requires the European countries to accept a certain number of refugees, with adequate EU funding per refugee to cover the settlement costs for the first two years. Additional funding from the EU and the United

States is also required to contribute funds to Jordan, Turkey, and Lebanon to help care for the refugees there.

Buddhist economics supports the efforts of the United Nations, and the push by people like George Soros, to provide care for the refugees fleeing war and climate devastation. Together, nations need to establish a system for dealing with forced migrations caused by violence, extreme weather, and food shortages. Panics and unnecessary human suffering must end.

CONCLUSION

Shared prosperity results from national policies that guide how our societies and economies work. Inequality, both domestically and globally, is a choice made by nations often without understanding how those at the top are using the system to enrich themselves and perpetuate their position. In Buddhist economics, shared prosperity around the world is a moral mandate.

Chapter 6

MEASURING QUALITY OF LIFE

*The demarcation between a positive and a negative
desire or action is not whether it gives you an immediate feeling of satisfaction but whether it ultimately
results in positive or negative consequences . . . One
interesting thing about greed is that although the
underlying motive is to seek satisfaction, the irony is
that even after obtaining the object of your desire, you
are still not satisfied.*

—DALAI LAMA, *THE ART OF HAPPINESS*

HOW WE MEASURE economic performance reflects our
values and guides us in how we live. Our economic goals
as individuals and as countries are intimately tied to the data
that we track and broadcast monthly. A Buddhist economic
system requires a measurement to evaluate how well the
economy is providing shared prosperity (distribution of
resources across families), sustainability (healthy ecosystems
now and for future generations), and quality of life (the well-
being of people living meaningful lives).

Today, countries around the world judge economic performance by tracking gross domestic product (GDP), which measures the market output of goods and services and by design equals national income. However, GDP ignores all activities outside the marketplace, and so it provides a lopsided and incomplete evaluation of economic performance. GDP is a calculation that fails at measuring our three major goals:

Quality of life. Only consumption of market goods and services is counted, and all other aspects of life are ignored.

Sustainability. Harm to the environment, such as air pollution, water pollution, or chemicals poured on the ground, is ignored.

Shared prosperity. The use of average GDP to indicate well-being ignores inequality. When incomes at the top increase, GDP per capita increases even as incomes of the nonrich remain stagnant.

Because economic growth has been captured by the rich, GDP growth is no longer a "rising tide that lifts all ships." Also, economic performance can no longer ignore environmental degradation and greenhouse gas emissions that are heating up the planet. We need a measurement that tracks people's ability to live a meaningful life in an equitable and sustainable world.

BEYOND GDP

As long as society is focused on what we buy and consume, our thinking and actions and government policy will be formed and then reinforced by the materialistic and individualistic measurement of GDP growth.

How can we measure economic performance so that it reflects our values, and lets us know whether our well-being is improving? We saw in Chapter 2 that over time, national happiness does not increase with national income (the Easterlin Paradox). What about more precise measures of social and economic well-being in developed countries? Here we see a difference in how average and relative income performs: national measures of health, education, and social problems (called quality of life indicators) do not improve with average national income, and so growth in national income (GDP) does not translate into increased national well-being. However, the national quality of life indicators do improve across countries as income inequality decreases. And if we look *within* a country, the distribution of income does matter: the quality of life indicators improve with people's income. This reinforces the Buddhist economics approach that cares whether low-income families have adequate income to buy basics, along with access to adequate health care, education, and social networks, so that all people collectively achieve their full potential.

Economic performance must also incorporate progress toward sustainability. Our planet cannot survive economic growth based on our fossil fuel economy. We've already seen the global problems caused by extreme weather and rising sea levels, and we must also factor in environmental degradation at the local level, where people's health is directly harmed by contaminated water, toxic soil, and polluted air in both rich and poor countries.

These results together tell us that the solution is to tie economic growth to improvements in equity, sustainability, and our nonmarket activities as well as to national income. Then we can measure economic performance in a holistic way across countries, and advanced countries will no longer be focused solely on average income growth. A holistic measure shows economic performance increasing when inequality goes down and the consumption of poorer families goes up, and when CO_2 emissions go down and the use of renewable energy sources goes up.

Once we begin to measure quality of life as integral to economic performance, we will set goals and develop policies that improve individual and national well-being rather than focus only on adding to income (especially consumption). Establishing a connection between economic performance and well-being encourages people to measure the progress of their lives and the progress of their economy in a more holistic and meaningful manner.

Yes, measuring economic performance in terms of quality of life is a tall order. But fortunately, Buddhist economics does not necessitate relearning everything we know about measuring economic performance. Economists already have ways to measure pollution and environmental damage, income inequality, happiness, human capabilities, and nonpaid activities (both useful and harmful). Around the world, broad measures of well-being have already been developed. Among them are Bhutan's Gross National Happiness Index, the UN's Human Development Index, the OECD (Organisation for Economic Co-operation and Development) Better Life Index, the Genuine Progress Indicator, and the Happy Planet Index. Below, we will use these measures as our guide in thinking how to create a measure of economic performance, but first we must better understand what the GDP tells us, and what it does not.

WHAT'S WRONG WITH THE GDP?

The GDP does have several things going for it as an economic measurement: How it is calculated is well understood (at least by economists), and it has been calculated in the same way by countries around the world for many years. Monthly measures of GDP allow us to compare economic (market) growth across countries and within a country. Countries have spent a great deal of time and money to improve how they measure national GDP, even though the Nobel laureate Simon Kuznets, who developed the GDP, warned in 1934 that it cannot be used to judge a country's welfare.

We are getting the wrong number right.

Because GDP uses only income to measure economic growth, income has become a country's primary focus. This encourages individuals to focus on what they buy and the country to pay little attention to inequality and sustainability, and the flawed measure of economic performance leads to flawed national policies that can lead us in the wrong direction.

So what does GDP growth tell us about the well-being of people? Certainly in the recovery of the GDP worldwide after the 2008 Great Recession, people in the United States and Europe didn't think their living standards were improving; their wages were stagnating, and the growth in jobs was a trickle.

When Hurricane Katrina destroyed much of New Orleans and the surrounding Gulf Coast in 2005, killing 1,833 people, GDP was not reduced by one penny. In fact, after the disaster struck, relief efforts costing over $120 billion and insurance payments of $41 billion were actually added to the GDP. So by this measure, the natural disaster helped the economy grow by

$161 billion—never mind the decline in quality of life for the residents of New Orleans or the thousands of people who have suffered for months and years as they have tried to rebuild their homes and lives.

Here is another example of how the GDP can be misleading. Let's compare a person who drives a Prius and gets 50 mpg to a neighbor who drives a Hummer and gets 14 mpg. Free market economics tells us that the Hummer is the better choice for the economy, because it adds more than three times what the Prius adds to the GDP for every mile driven. Since the GDP records only the gas bought, and ignores the harm caused by the CO_2 emissions, the GDP drives us to an illogical conclusion.

In a Buddhist economic system, the cost of the pollution is included in the price of gasoline, and the negative environmental impact is included in the measurement of economic performance; thus, using less gas per mile driven has a beneficial effect on economic performance. By charging for emissions and exacting an economic price for pollution, the system creates incentives for people to buy more fuel-efficient vehicles, for car companies to make and sell them, for localities to provide better options for public transportation, and for innovators to come up with creative transportation alternatives, such as car sharing.

Here's a cheat sheet on how to calculate Buddhist measures of economic performance:

- Increasing consumption of basic goods adds to economic performance, but more consumption of status goods does not.
- Involuntary unemployment subtracts from economic performance, and increased time for nonmarket

activities—that is, unpaid activities outside the marketplace—adds to it.

- Environmental degradation subtracts from economic performance, and consuming clean energy adds to it.
- Declines in health have a negative effect, while improvements in education have a positive one.
- Improving the opportunities available to each person adds to the economy; crime, violence, and natural disasters subtract from the economy.
- Mindful use of time for work, family, and community increases economic performance, and overwork or harmful activities decrease growth.
- Overall, growth is measured in terms of the mindful use of resources, which includes restoring and nurturing the sources of those goods, while harmful and wasteful consumption decreases growth.

These are commonsense ways to evaluate the economy and how well we live, and they should be the monthly measures that guide the Federal Reserve Bank and Congress in their policies. Because they measure, and thereby value, quality of life much more broadly than does the GDP, they offer a pathway to prosperity for all, and a sustainable one at that.

THREE HOLISTIC WAYS TO MEASURE ECONOMIC PERFORMANCE

Now that we see the things we need to include in a holistic measure, we can turn to the difficult task of actually creating that measure.

Holistic measurements of economic performance are usually calculated in three ways: a single-value measure (in terms of dollars or other currency) based on government data; a nondollar index, usually based on survey data and often presented as a percentage; and a dashboard that presents many indicators (often relative to other countries) based on a variety of data sources. Each has its strengths and weaknesses, and each is useful for understanding different aspects of economic performance.

1. The *single-value measure* expands on GDP by adding in the value of nonmarket benefits (e.g., child rearing, leisure) and subtracting the value of nonmarket costs (e.g., environmental degradation, depletion of natural capital), and also adjusting for inequality across the population. Because all components are given a monetary value, they can be added together to provide a single value for quality of life, which indicates a country's economic performance over time. This measure also allows us to inspect how the individual components, such as environmental degradation or distribution of consumption, are trending. In order to compare economic performance across countries, all countries would have to use the same technique to measure quality of life, just as they do now for the GDP. The Genuine Progress Indicator is the most commonly used single-value measure, but no country has taken the lead in coordinating its adoption. (More on the GPI later.)

2. The *nondollar index* provides us with one overall index that aggregates variables that have *not* been transformed into dollar (or any other currency) values. Instead, the variables are transformed to the same scale (often 0 to 10) and then aggregated according to

a specific method to form an overall index. The nondollar indices use a variety of methods to aggregate their wide array of variables. A well-known example of a nondollar index is Bhutan's Gross National Happiness (GNH) Index, which is a complex summation of nine equal domains—psychological well-being, use of time, community vitality, cultural diversity, ecological resilience, standard of living, health, education, and good governance. A person's happiness score can range from 0 to 100 percent. The domains are calculated from a total of 33 indicators, which themselves are aggregates of 124 weighted survey variables with lower weights attached to more subjective variables. Then a sufficiency level is assigned to each domain. The GNH provides a measure of policy outcomes that shows how many people reach sufficiency in each of the domains.

Using the GNH, Bhutan surveyed its entire population in 2010 to create each person's "happiness" score, and then surveyed a sample representing the entire country in 2015. Its goal was to understand how people with different levels of education or employment and in different regions vary by their scores, in order to improve the conditions of "not-yet-happy" people (9 percent of the population) and also "narrowly happy" people (48 percent). Bhutan learned that urban dwellers are happier than people living in isolated rural areas, and that monks and highly educated persons reported being "extremely happy."

Another way to aggregate variables into a nondollar index is to set each country's value relative to other countries' values for each component, and then aggregate those into a single index (valued between 0 and 1) that shows the relative ranking of countries. An example is the widely used Human Development Index

(HDI), which has been calculated for up to 187 countries since 1990. Its three dimensions are health (life expectancy), education (mean and expected years of schooling), and living standards (income per capita). The index for each country is calculated, and a country's relative rank, but not its absolute change, can be compared across years. However, the HDI does not include adjustments for inequality or for environmental degradation.

3. The *dashboard* provides a variety of indicators of well-being without aggregating them into one overall value. Each indicator is usually based upon many variables, including subjective survey data and objective government data, that are considered essential in providing specific goals for well-being. The indicators are presented separately, and so we see only how each is trending over time. Because the dashboard is not aggregated into one overall measure of well-being, it does not show how the national quality of life changes over time.

Often the dashboard of indicators is calculated for a group of countries relative to one another. Then each indicator shows the ranking of countries. The downside of this relative approach is that we cannot tell, for example, whether all countries together are doing better for a single indicator, such as quality of environment. The OECD Better Life Index (BLI) is this type of measurement, and we will look at it in more detail later.

GETTING THE RIGHT NUMBER

Countries and experts don't agree on how to measure quality of life, reflecting their differences of opinion about how to prioritize social and economic goals and about how well a specific measure captures these goals. No one method has been accepted as the metric of choice. Even those who agree to use a specific approach continue to debate over what variables to include and how to calculate them. Advocates for health care, the poor, or the environment often disagree because the indicator they care about may be lost in a quality of life dashboard, and that particular indicator certainly would not be front and center in a single measure. Disagreements also abound as to the quality of the data used to measure many of the variables. Some argue that we must use objective data collected on measurements of actual outcomes, such as water quality, health problems, and crime. Others want to use people's perceptions (subjective data) about their water quality, health, and safety, not to mention happiness.

We must address all these concerns in order to generate a consensus on how to move beyond the GDP to measure quality of life. We can agree that no "perfect" measure exists, and we will decide what metrics to use globally to measure and compare quality of life across countries in the years ahead. Certainly, even imperfect measures will do a better job than does the GDP. Also, once a measure is used worldwide, experience can guide experts in improving that measure. After all, the GDP was developed with refinements made over decades.

Measuring Progress in Poor and Rich Countries

Some measures are better suited for poor countries and some for rich countries because of the vast differences in their living standards and needs. Poor countries have to meet basic needs, such as food and water, shelter, health care, and education, while rich countries have to meet the basic needs of those at the bottom, especially to ensure jobs with living wages, and also to improve quality of life for everyone in nonmaterial ways, such as providing for balanced lives with time for family and friends, less stress, and better eating and exercise habits. All countries, regardless of income, can improve quality of life by improving the well-being of their poorest people and restoring the health of degraded ecosystems.

The widely used Human Development Index (HDI) was created by the United Nations as a way to evaluate well-being in poor countries based on improvements in life expectancy, literacy, and income. A poor country's HDI indicates performance in these three areas relative to other countries. The HDI is less useful for evaluating rich countries because rich countries always come out on top, with longer life expectancies, more education, and higher incomes. This point is starkly illustrated in Figure 3, which plots the HDI to national income per person. The two increase together, as we would expect, because income is part of the HDI. What is notable here is that the rich countries have more variation in income than in the HDI, while poor countries have more variation in the HDI than in income.

Rich countries' high HDI scores are shown by the dots running up the graph on the right (see page 115), which shows their income spread. Almost all 49 countries awarded the UN category of "very high human development" (an HDI of 0.80 to 0.94) have an average per person income of above $20,000. The poor countries are spread out along the bottom of the graph, which shows their variation in HDI scores over their low incomes. Life

expectancy and education drive the HDI scores for poor countries because their incomes are so low. Most of the 43 countries
with the UN grade of "low human development" (an HDI of
0.33 to 0.55) have average incomes per person of less than $5,000.

To measure and compare the quality of life in rich countries,
we can use a single-value measure such as the Genuine Progress
Indicator (GPI), which incorporates income inequality, nonmarket activities, and the environment as well as market consumption. But although the GPI is a good measure for showing
how richer countries differ in their holistic economic performance, consumption per person in poor countries is so low that
the GPIs are very low and in a similar range. One study of the

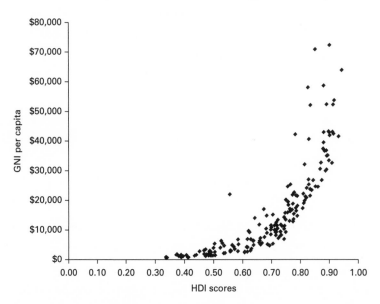

Figure 3: GNI vs HDI (2013). Gross National Income per capita in PPP
$2011. Three small oil-rich countries with GNI above $80,000 (Qatar,
Kuwait, and Liechtenstein) are not shown. Recall that GNI is a component
of HDI. Source: Calculated from 2014 UN Human Development Report,
http://hdr.undp.org/en/data.

GPIs of seventeen countries shows that the GPI per person for industrialized countries varied widely between the years 1990 and 2005 (for example, it ranged from $7,500 to $17,000 for the United States, Japan, and the UK) but varied hardly at all for people in poorer countries (for example, it hovered around $2,000 for China, India, and Vietnam throughout those fifteen years).

As you can see, using the same method to measure quality of life for both rich and poor countries in a meaningful way is tricky.

Measuring Happiness

One popular measure used across all countries is life satisfaction, often called happiness. Many psychologists and economists put happiness at the top of the list when discussing how to measure well-being across all countries and peoples.

What happens when we ask people if they are happy or satisfied with life?

Recall the two types of happiness: *hedonic happiness*, which comes from pleasure without pain, along with life satisfaction; and *eudaimonic happiness*, which comes from living a worthwhile life. Surveys of people's evaluation of their own well-being measures their hedonic happiness. People are asked about their life satisfaction, based on their self-chosen standards, and also about their short-term feelings of pleasure or pain.

A widely used measure of hedonic happiness or well-being is the Cantril Ladder, which is collected annually by the Gallup organization for more than 150 countries. People report where they feel they stand on a ladder, at this time, that goes from the bottom step (0, worst possible life) to the top step (10, best possible life).

Should this measure of happiness become the defining yard-stick of human welfare?

There is no easy answer to that question, as the Cantril Ladder is no more perfect than the other yardsticks examined here. Asking people in extremely poor countries—people who do not have adequate food, water, shelter, health care, and education—about their happiness won't provide us with much information about their well-being. Poor people do the best they can with the opportunities they have, which may be constrained by race, gender, sexual orientation, and family background as well as by the country where they are born. For these people, objectively measuring their consumption and basic capabilities tells us much more. As two researchers noted, measuring well-being becomes "capabilities for the miserable; happiness for the satisfied."

The Cantril Ladder of happiness also leaves a lot to be desired in Buddhist economics, because it does not tell us how people are actually living and caring for one another. We need to know how they are behaving, not just how they are feeling, if we are to gain more insight into whether they are living mean-ingful and joyful lives. After all, Buddhism teaches us to focus on the good aspects of life with gratitude and not complaints.

In a nonpoor country, where the resources to meet basic needs are available to most, asking people how satisfied they feel about their lives does provide a subjective measure of happi-ness, but that measure is influenced by culture. For example, in Japan it is considered bad manners to say you are doing better than others ("the nail sticking up gets hammered down"), while in the United States, a person often proudly declares that he is doing better than others, and doing more than his share.

And then there is the issue of how, on the Cantril Ladder of life satisfaction, we interpret what a score of 10 or 6 or 0 means, or compare a 6 to a 7 score, when people are using their own standards of happiness, which are embedded in social norms.

However, the Cantril Ladder does show a wide range of scores for a mix of rich and poor countries over a period of time. Happiness scores (average Cantril Ladder scores) for 157 countries from 2013 through 2015 ranged from 2.9 for Burundi to 7.5 for Denmark. Also on the plus side, the Cantril Ladder does a good job of tracking other variables considered important, such as income per person, having someone to count on in times of trouble, healthy life expectancy at birth, and satisfied with freedom to make key life choices.

Buddhist economics cares about shared prosperity, and so we want to know how happiness is distributed within a country and across countries. On a happiness index like the Cantril Ladder, everyone can report the same score, because an increase in one person's happiness does not come from a decrease in another person's happiness. Our earlier measure of inequality, the Gini coefficient, doesn't tell us much because complete equality (Gini=0) means that everyone reports the same happiness score. Equality could mean everyone is perfectly happy (10), or everyone is deeply unhappy (0), or everyone is moderately happy (5), then you have equality. From 2010 to 2012, the Gini of happiness was between 0.15 and 0.23, which is more equal than the Gini coefficients for disposable income (see Figure 2, Chapter 5).

We see that in nonpoor countries, people's self-reported happiness scores are much more alike, and so indicate less inequality, than objective measures such as income or health outcomes. This happens because people are very resilient and learn to do the best they can with their situation in life.

For example, let's compare the average happiness scores and average income per person for the OECD countries. Most of the 34 industrialized countries in the OECD have an average life satisfaction score between 6.5 and 7.5. Their average per capita income is much more spread out, with 9 of the countries in a middle range ($30,000 to $40,000 GDP per person), 14 in a high range ($40,000 to $85,000), and 11 in a low range ($16,000 to $30,000) in 2014. Nations are much more equal in their average happiness than in their average incomes.

Proponents of using the Cantril Ladder as a universal measure of well-being or happiness have examined the inequality of happiness within countries as measured by the statistical variation in the Cantril Ladder scores (called the standard deviation). They found that the inequality of happiness varies across countries according to life circumstances, and a country's inequality of happiness has a negative impact on its average happiness.

Buddhist economics also cares about making everyone happy and reducing suffering. We can measure the distribution of happiness by comparing the happiness scores of the least happy people (bottom 10 percent) to the scores of the most happy people (top 10 percent). The higher the ratio, the more equal is everyone's happiness. Figure 4 shows the inequality of happiness in twenty countries. Typically, people in the bottom 10 percent have happiness scores about half as high as those in the top 10 percent. Two countries, Denmark and the Netherlands, stand out as having happiness distributed fairly equally—the least happy people's scores indicate they are 60 percent as happy as the most happy people. China has the most unequal happiness, with the least happy people's scores indicating they are only 25 percent as happy as the most happy people. The lesson here is that countries may appear similar in their average happiness, but they vary in how happiness is distributed across the population. No matter how we slice it, however, happiness appears to be much more equally distributed than income.

Economists also look at how a country's happiness score changes over time to see whether people are becoming happier, or not. Happiness scores change slowly. Periods of crisis, such as a natural disaster or war, cause national happiness to decline for a time, but then it tends to return to its previous level.

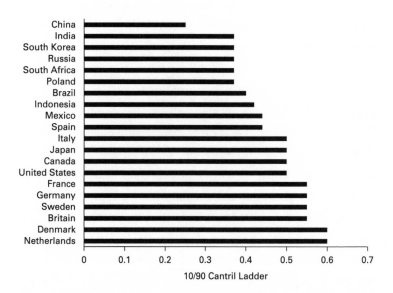

Figure 4: Inequality in Happiness, 2010. The 10/90 Cantril Ladder shows the score of the least satisfied (bottom 10 percent) divided by the score of the most satisfied (top 10 percent, who are above 90 percent). Source: Calculated from http://www.economist.com/blogs/dailychart/2011/10 /inequality-and-happiness.

You might ask if it would help to use eudaimonic happiness as a yardstick for well-being, but this approach suffers from the same problems as any happiness measure. Even proponents of eudaimonic happiness wonder how to measure it. Some surveys ask people if their life has purpose or meaning, and if they consider their daily activities to be worthwhile. Most agree that eudaimonic happiness includes meaningful social relationships, and surveys often ask if a person's social relationships are supportive and rewarding. Since Buddhist economics emphasizes helping others and relieving suffering, one way to expand the "worthwhile life" survey is to ask if the person actively contributes to the happiness and well-being of others. Once again, however, social values influence answers, and the idea of a "worthwhile" life may seem like bragging to someone who is striving to be connected with others and squash their ego.

Wondering about how to measure and interpret happiness brings us to the question: Can our measure of economic performance be used to evaluate policies? We want to use a metric of well-being that allows us to evaluate the dramatic changes in our economic system required to prevent the destruction of our ecosystems and spread prosperity from rich to poor nations. Current surveys of happiness such as the Cantril Ladder won't help us predict how people will feel about life under policies that are meant to restructure and transform daily activities. Happiness may soar for those who love nature and hate shopping, but plummet for those who love SUVs and flying around the world. We only know that happiness may decline with new policies, but not long after the new policies are implemented, we should expect happiness to return to its previous level.

Factoring In Sustainability

The Cantril Ladder ignores the issue of sustainability. To fill this gap, we turn to the Happy Planet Index (HPI), which measures a country's Happy Life Years (the Cantril Ladder score times life expectancy, both adjusted for inequality) divided by its ecological footprint (the amount of land required per person to replicate the country's consumption over time). This provides a single measure of a nation's happiness, health, sustainability, and inequality, without including income. The HPI 2016 shows how 140 countries are ranked, with scores ranging from a high of 44.7 for Costa Rica to a low of 12.8 for Chad. But all these scores are low, and they tell us that the planet is not happy—that economic activity as we know it is not sustainable.

The Happy Planet Index shows rich countries are overusing global resources to support their extravagant lifestyles. Rich countries do well at producing long and happy lives for most people, but at enormous environmental cost. Their ecological footprints are three to five times the 1.73 footprint that is compatible with sustainability. The eighteen high-income countries ($40,000 annual income per person) have high scores for life expectancy and happiness, but only the United Kingdom has an ecological footprint under 5.0—still way above being sustainable. The United States' HPI is a low 20.7 (rank 108 out of 140) because its footprint is a high 8.2 (rank 4). Each person in the United States requires more than eight global hectares, or almost *five times* the sustainable level.

Poorer countries have much lower ecological footprints, but their longevity and happiness scores are also lower. Only forty-six countries have a sustainable footprint (under 1.7). One half of them have extremely low incomes ($1,000 per person annually), and only five of them have incomes above $3,000 per person annually. These sustainable economic systems produce a wide range of outcomes for life expectancy and happiness; their happy life years range from 9.0 for Togo to 32.8 for Vietnam.

A comparison of the HPI for India and China points out the difficulty of improving the standard of living in a sustainable economic system. India's HPI is 29.2 (rank 50), which reflects her low life expectancy (51.1, rank 100) and happiness score (4.2, rank 100), both brought down by adjusting for high inequality, and then brought up by a low sustainable footprint (1.2). China's HPI (25.7, rank 72) is even lower than India's HPI, because China's higher life expectancy (68.6, rank 48) and happiness score (4.6, rank 74), are brought down by their intermediate inequality, and reduced further by an unsustainable footprint of 3.4. China and India have large numbers of extremely poor people, around 400 million in India and 150 million in China, and these people are in desperate need of more food, clean water, sanitation, and shelter, not to mention education and decent jobs. Unless we help India and China develop without using fossil fuels, we know their HPI score will decline as their footprint grows.

The Happy Planet Index incorporates sustainability, happiness, health, and inequality, but it does not take into consideration the daily activities that create a meaningful life, and so we are still left pondering how to measure well-being in Buddhist economics.

So let's look at two broader measures being used, the Genuine Progress Indicator and the Better Life Index. Both measure quality of life.

THE GENUINE PROGRESS INDICATOR AND THE
BETTER LIFE INDEX

A quality of life measure for developed countries must combine
all aspects of life that we value: our health, families and communities, knowledge and skills, work, development as individuals,
helping others, political participation, safety, and the ecosystem.
To do so, the Genuine Progress Indicator (GPI) uses a single-
value measurement, and the Better Life Index (BLI) uses a
dashboard of indicators. The GPI assigns prices to the things
we value, such as consumption, housework, democratic participation, and environmental conservation. The BLI uses surveys
that ask people their perceptions about their lives, health, and
government. To help us decide which method we'd like to use,
let's look in detail at how the GPI and BLI are calculated and
how they describe quality of life today.

The Genuine Progress Indicator combines twenty-six indicators to measure economic, social, and environmental well-
being with one number. National GPI has been estimated for
many countries, and we have consistent estimates of GPI for the
period 1950–2003 for seventeen countries.

The GPI begins with people's market consumption and
adjusts it for inequality. Then it adds the value of nonmarket
activities and public goods and services, and subtracts the value
of environmental degradation. The GPI is calculated from over
two dozen variables in the following way:

Personal consumption adjusted for inequality (using the
      Gini coefficient),
plus the value of nonmarket work (such as child care and
      housework),

lue of leisure (adjusted for unemployment) and
'r work,

goods (such as health care, education, roads
and parks),

minus defensive expenditures (such as crime and commuting, that reduce quality of life),

minus environmental impact (including depletion of natural capital, CO_2 emissions, and water pollution).

The GPI directly incorporates inequality by adjusting consumption for income inequality using the Gini coefficient in order to tell us how well our economy is providing market goods and services to *all* families. Adjusting consumption for inequality decreases the GPI when inequality is increasing, and thus the GPI indicates a worsening of economic performance. For example, if we don't adjust the GPI for inequality, then U.S. GPI grew steadily over the twenty-five years from 1980 to 2004, with some minor ups and downs, as U.S. income (GDP) per person grew. But as income inequality grew, family consumption did not keep up with income growth, and so the GPI grew less than the GDP.

When a country is using up nonrenewable resources and emitting greenhouse gases, this reduces GPI as well. For all industrialized countries, GPI falls below GDP because of their negative environmental impact. Putting values on environmental factors is challenging in measuring quality of life. How to value the impact of human activity on our ecosystems is not straightforward when the planet's systems are near threshold boundaries (as discussed in Chapter 4). Today, the values the GPI uses for natural capital assume that we can use natural

capital as we wish (weak sustainability). When we preserve crit
ical levels for many natural resources (strong sustainability), then
actual values become infinite if the limit is reached. Experts
disagree on how much damage our critical ecosystems can
sustain before collapsing, but in calculating the GPI, we must
consider how to incorporate strong sustainability, perhaps by
using the ecological footprint. At the very least, we can add a red
light that goes on if any critical ecosystem becomes threatened.

The Genuine Progress Indicator tells us how quality of life is
going up or down over time, especially in terms of consumption and nonmarket activities, equality, and sustainability. The
GPI is especially useful in evaluating policies that are designed
to reduce inequality, mitigate global warming, stop depleting
natural capital, or reduce work hours. Although the improvements that the policies bring about may not be evident within a
year or two, their impact can be simulated through the GPI to
see what is likely to happen a decade or so later.

But what if we care about human rights, social support systems,
or caring for others? The GPI includes our leisure time and our
volunteer work, and our health care expenditures; it subtracts for
crime and commute time. But still it leaves out other noneco-
nomic aspects of life that are crucial in Buddhist economics.

This brings us to the alternative approach of a dashboard of
indicators, such as the OECD Better Life Index, which compares
the quality of life across countries by calculating their relative
rankings for eleven indicators: income, jobs, community, education, housing, environment, governance, health, life satisfaction,
safety, and work-life balance. This approach allows us to evaluate nonmarket aspects of life that are important to us. The
downside is that we end up with an array of indicators and have

to prioritize them and make our own decisions about whether
a country's well-being is improving or not as we look at one
indicator at a time. We also cannot use the BLI to evaluate
improvements in a country's quality of life from year to year.

The eleven indicators in the Better Life Index (values
between 0 and 10) are based upon twenty-four variables that
include both objective survey measures, such as education and
unemployment, and subjective measures, such as people's opinions about their life satisfaction or water quality. The BLI is
presented only as the eleven indicators that show the ranking of
the thirty-four OECD countries, with no aggregation of the
indicators into one number. Inequality (the Gini coefficient) is
shown as a supplementary indicator, and it is not directly incorporated into the BLI indicators.

Figure 5 shows us two BLI indicators that are now familiar to
you—income and life satisfaction. What pops out is that income
and satisfaction don't show much of a relationship in these industrialized countries. The good news is that twelve countries (in
Northern Europe, North America, Australia, and New Zealand)
have high relative satisfaction (0.8 to 1.0) and only three (Greece,
Hungary, and Turkey) have low satisfaction (considerably below
0.2). The bad news is that ten countries (in Eastern Europe and
South America) have low relative income (below 0.2) and the
United States has very high relative income (above 0.8).

An alternative way to create a dashboard that uses data similar
to the BLI is the United Kingdom Well-Being Measures. This
dashboard shows how the UK (or its regions) is doing over time
(one indicator at a time), because it does not convert the indicators
into relative rankings as the OECD dashboard does. The UK
Well-Being Measures has ten indicators that track forty-one

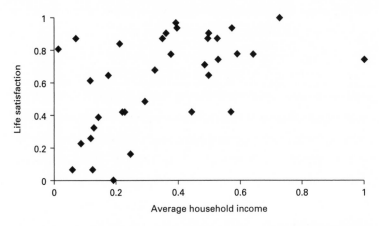

Figure 5: Life Satisfaction and Income Indicators for OECD Countries, 2014. Life satisfaction is the Cantril Ladder and average household income combines disposable income (after taxes and transfers) and net financial wealth. Both indicators are adjusted to be between 0 and 1 to show the relative ranking of the countries. Source: Calculated from OECD Better Life Index, http://www.oecdbetterlifeindex.org/.

variables over time. Now we are left to ponder how forty-one variables fit together to measure quality of life. Even the indicator "personal well-being" has five measures of happiness. No wonder people want to fall back onto a single subjective measure like the Cantril Ladder to represent national well-being.

Another measurement system is now in the works to evaluate how well a country has satisfied the UN's Sustainable Development Goals (SDG) for 147 countries. This project, led by Jeffrey Sachs, presents a dashboard of data for the seventeen development goals, then aggregates the goals into one measurement for each country. The SDG index and dashboard look promising as a way in which to evaluate how well countries are advancing in improving quality of life in a Buddhist economic system.

On an unhappy note, we have conveniently left out war

and violence from all our indices. War kills and maims people and endangers the environment. War destroys people's homes and towns and creates waves of refugees desperately searching for a safe place to live. Yet war's environmental degradation is not included in measures of GHG emissions, and no dollar measure of personal well-being can adequately capture the harm and suffering created by war and violence.

CONCLUSION

In looking at how to measure economic performance, our goal is to find a way to measure quality of life, along with sustainability and shared prosperity. No perfect measure exists. Instead we have a plethora of measures that do a good job of evaluating quality of life in either poor or rich countries, or of evaluating specific aspects of well-being such as basic consumption, health, education, human rights, and social networks. While the many alternative metrics are competing with each other to measure economic performance holistically, the GDP continues to be used worldwide to evaluate well-being.

Buddhist economics wants to go beyond the GDP and use other measures in a way that helps people and nations create more meaningful, sustainable lives worldwide. To do this, we need to use a single-value measure, such as the GPI, to replace the GDP as the measure of economic performance over years and across countries. Government leaders and central banks need to have one measure to guide budgetary and monetary policies. The media needs to have one number to report each month to let viewers know how the economy is performing.

We know that a single measure valued in dollars, such as the

GPI, cannot include all aspects of a meaningful life, such as human rights and freedoms, good governance, or even happiness. Also, the GPI is not an adequate indicator of well-being in poor countries, whose market consumption is very low. For these reasons, the GPI should be supplemented with other indicators. For emerging countries, we suggest supplementing the single-value measure with the HDI. To evaluate specific nonmarket goals, including happiness, we can use dashboards such as the Better Life Index or the Sustainable Development Goals Index. Together the GPI and the specific measures can be used to evaluate policies that are being advocated by politicians and others.

Because our survival demands that the environment be protected, we must also track the extent to which any of Earth's critical ecosystems are being threatened. For example, a country's ecological footprint can indicate if its use of resources is sustainable, and the United Nations can use red flags to warn us when Earth is approaching the boundary threshold of an ecosystem and can then oversee the immediate action to be taken by all countries.

Once countries agree to set and use the identical single-value metric to measure economic performance as quality of life, then each country can decide individually what dashboard of indicators to measure and use to evaluate the goals most important to them.

With countries around the world using a holistic measure of economic performance, along with indicators for specific social and political goals, we have the metrics needed to guide us in the transformation to a Buddhist economy.

Now we turn to the steps to create a more sustainable and prosperous future. Let's leap forward to a Buddhist economy.

Chapter 7

LEAP TO BUDDHIST ECONOMICS

> *The forces of greed, exploitation and over-consumption seem to have overwhelmed our economies in recent decades. Our materialistic societies offer us little choice but to exploit and compete for survival in today's dog-eat-dog world. But at the same time, it is obvious that these forces are damaging our societies and ravaging our environment.*
>
> —PAYUTTO, *BUDDHIST ECONOMICS*

OUR MATERIALISTIC AND wasteful carbon-based global economy has created enormous inequality, with lavish lifestyles for those at the top and desperate lives for those at the bottom. Our relentless pursuit of economic growth and consumption has plundered the environment and sickened the earth, our common home.

It is time to start a dialogue about how to move to a Buddhist economy. For the planet, and for ourselves, there's no time to lose.

Buddhist economics guides us in how to create a sustainable economy that provides a meaningful life to everyone. This chapter outlines steps that nations and individuals can take to achieve these lofty goals. Together we can undertake a wide variety of activities at the individual, community, national, and global levels to mitigate global warming and dramatically improve global welfare for people and Nature.

Human prosperity and planetary stability are both possible. The transition to a low-carbon economy is achievable and affordable, and it will come with extensive economic and health benefits.

To make sense of the myriad ways that political action, economic forces, and technology can be used to mitigate global warming and share global prosperity, we look now at eight crucial steps to transform the world to Buddhist economics. I hear your arguments that these are not the "best" eight steps and that the details are not right (and indeed, some might be wrong). The point is not to determine the perfect process today, but to start a dialogue about how to move to a Buddhist economy in order to save the earth and its inhabitants from human destruction and to live mindfully with one another and Earth to be happy.

These eight steps are not meant to mirror the Buddhist Eightfold Path, but to provide guidelines as to what countries, companies, and people can do to create meaningful life on a healthy planet.

The first four steps are for nations, the next two for companies, and the final two for each of us. Here they are:

1. Tax and transfer
2. Sustainable agriculture
3. Measure and transform

4. Peace and prosperity
5. Green production and green products
6. Living wages and balanced lives
7. Live mindfully with love, compassion, and wisdom
8. Work together and take action

I. TAX AND TRANSFER

Well-structured markets are an important part of Buddhist economics. We know that free markets don't exist and that unregulated markets can produce unacceptable outcomes, except for the few businesses that control them. Companies and the rich have been creating market rules to maintain their power and wealth for the past four decades. Now governments must restructure markets with new regulations and taxes that will create a sustainable global economy that works for everyone's benefit. We need markets that provide incentives for people and companies to make decisions that will support our ecosystems and distribute resources equitably.

The government role of "tax and transfer" includes all government actions that structure markets and economic activities to achieve our goals. This is our biggest and most complex step in making the leap to Buddhist economics. This step includes four actions that nations around the world can take to tackle the critical challenges of global warming and inequality: (a) tax and regulate carbon and consumption; (b) share prosperity at home; (c) keep fossil fuel reserves in the ground; and (d) share green technology to create prosperity around the world.

In order for governments to play the leading role in bringing about change, people must trust them to be honest and to work in the country's best interests. Government leaders must not be beholden to the business leaders and investment bankers who have provided the money for their expensive election campaigns. Also, in tackling the looming climate catastrophe, governments and central banks must be willing to develop policies that would extend over many decades. They must not fall victim to focusing only on the next business or political cycle.

Tax and Regulate Carbon and Consumption

Let's start with taxes on carbon and on consumption, which would fight both global warming and income inequality. Global warming is harming poor people and poor countries more than the rich and thus exacerbating inequality. Today economic justice and environmental justice have converged at home and around the world.

Carbon taxes make the market price of fossil fuels reflect the damage of CO_2 emissions, now and in the future. Most economists, free market and Buddhist alike, agree that a carbon tax is required to accelerate the transition to a carbon-free world. Some forty national governments and more than twenty states and localities have started pricing some carbon pollution, and the IMF and World Bank are pushing nations to create a carbon tax. Nonetheless, the fossil fuel companies still receive billions of dollars in government subsidies that reduce fossil fuel prices, lower exploration and exploitation costs, and increase after-tax profits.

Think of a subsidy as a negative tax: society ends up paying a "tax" that subsidizes a company's costs. In this case, the tax on society is the pollution and the degradation of ecosystems.

Countries even provide direct subsidies to fossil fuel companies, such as tax breaks. For this reason, in 2009 the OECD countries agreed to phase out their fossil fuel subsidies. The OECD tracks their progress, and while subsidies are steadily declining, the pace is too slow. In 2014, the forty countries paid out $160 billion in fossil fuel subsidies.

The IMF estimates that direct fossil fuel subsidies for all countries together were $333 billion in 2015. But here is the truly shocking number: once environmental damage, health problems, and other social costs are factored in, the total subsidies shoot up to $5.3 trillion, or 6.5 percent of global economic output for 2015. In developing Asian countries, the costs are mostly from local air pollution, especially that caused by the use of coal and diesel, and only one fourth comes from climate change. The quality of life in these countries, especially in terms of the people's health, would be greatly improved by ending the use of coal.

The price of oil and gas has always been volatile, and this cripples planning by the country and by the consumer. To keep the price of oil and gasoline steady, governments can increase the price of fossil fuels with a carbon tax that moves inversely with the price of oil and gas. This keeps the price high to incorporate the social costs and keeps the price steady to help economic planning.

Unfortunately, the question of how to use the revenue—the "transfer" part of "tax and transfer"—from taxes on carbon is hotly debated. The Buddhist economics approach would use the revenues to help the needy at home and around the world. Taxes on carbon would allow governments to rebate the revenue to the people so that they could afford the higher price of fuels or even better to reward those who are using less energy. Alaska is already doing this.

One inclusive program is "cap and dividend," advocated by the entrepreneur and writer Peter Barnes. The program taxes a broad range of income sources from public wealth, including fees charged for carbon emissions, securities transactions, intellectual property protection, and use of the electromagnetic spectrum, with the revenue distributed equally to everyone. He estimates that this plan would generate a $5,000 dividend to each adult and child in the United States, with the carbon tax portion alone remitting about $1,000 per person. Clearly a win-win for the earth and humanity.

Some countries, including Germany, France, and the United States, have successfully reduced emissions with regulations, which are a critical tool to complement a carbon tax; they can also stand alone. Regulations on industry greenhouse gas emissions, on automobile miles-per-gallon requirements, and on water pollution have resulted in cleaner air and water, and in better environmental performance by companies overall. A major U.S. study shows that between 1990 and 2008, emissions of major regulated air pollutants from U.S. manufacturers fell by 60 percent, even as manufacturing output grew substantially. The observed reduction in air pollutants was largely the result of more stringent environmental regulations over this time period.

Meanwhile, consumption taxes, especially taxes on luxuries, can reduce inequality. Consumption taxes, which buyers cannot dodge, are already in place in many countries in Asia and Europe as value-added taxes, although these taxes are not always designed to be progressive. Progressive taxes on the top earners' income and wealth, as well as on luxury purchases, could be used to provide transfers to low-income families.

Taxing carbon and consumption are government programs that would provide incentives for firms to invest in and use renewable energy, and for people to live a lifestyle that does not flaunt their status or ravage the earth. Tax and transfer programs provide for shared prosperity with reduced suffering at the bottom and less isolation at the top.

Share Prosperity at Home

Rich countries have a menu of tax and transfer options to choose from to create a more equal income distribution. Such programs need to be broad and substantial. Here is a short list of income redistribution policies being touted by eminent economists today: (i) A guaranteed minimum income, which provides a safety net for all. This policy has a long history, being proposed and attacked by both conservatives and liberals in the United States. Today, my popular colleague Robert Reich advocates a version of this program that would pay adults a minimum income from patent profits. (ii) Providing a capital endowment to young people at adulthood, so that they have a chance to finance their education or make investments in their future, just as rich kids do (with lots more money). (iii) Employee ownership and profit sharing, another policy with a long history, now being advocated by the Harvard economist Richard Freeman. He favors using the program as a way for workers to receive some of the company's income from capital. The companies then benefit from worker loyalty and higher productivity—a win-win approach for both workers and companies.

But even if countries do find their way to creating shared prosperity at home, will there be prosperity to share if we overheat the earth?

Keep It in the Ground

Environmental activists chant "Keep it in the ground" to remind us that we must keep fossil fuels in the ground. More than 80 percent of current coal reserves, half of gas reserves, and a third of oil reserves must remain in the ground to stay under the 2°C target for global warming. Yet the United States has dramatically increased its fossil fuel reserves by fracking, a method that combines hydraulic fracturing and horizontal drilling for the extraction of oil and natural gas. The upside of fracking is that the United States is now much less dependent on the Middle East for energy, consumers pay lower prices for gasoline and home heating, fossil fuel company profits are down, and phasing out coal-powered plants has become cheaper and more feasible. The downside is that most of the "new" reserves made possible by fracking cannot be developed without overheating the earth. The United States can lead the way to "Keep it in the ground" by outlawing the extraction of fossil fuels on government-owned lands, which contain up to one half of all remaining fossil fuel reserves in the United States.

Don't be fooled by the natural gas industry's push to expand the use of natural gas as the "clean" fossil fuel that can be the bridge that takes us from coal to renewable energy. Most people don't know that natural gas is mostly methane (CH_4), a greenhouse gas. Natural gas is *not* clean energy because of the high leakage of methane at wellheads, along pipelines, and from fracking. The extraction and transport of natural gas has resulted in an enormous leakage of invisible methane into the atmosphere. Most of the methane leaks are not measured or counted in greenhouse gas emissions, but you can see the methane in the air in California and the southwestern United States at http://sanfrancisco.cbslocal.com/2014/10/09 /mysterious-sources-of-methane-viewed-from-space-makes -central-california-2nd-worst-hot-spot-in-nation-agriculture- nasa-global-warming-fresno-livestock/.

We know that implementing a carbon tax is important if we are to create the right price incentives. However, a post-carbon economy also requires direct action in three other areas:

- Replace fossil fuel with renewable energy to produce clean electricity;
- Use clean electricity to power vehicles and provide heating; and
- Improve energy efficiency in industry, buildings, machines, and transportation systems, and reduce energy waste.

These goals require governments to make large-scale investments in public infrastructure and to subsidize renewable energy.

At COP21, most industrialized countries embraced the so-called 80/50 goal: to reduce greenhouse gas emissions to at least 80 percent below their 1990 level by 2050. Reaching 80/50 is possible to do with existing technology, and the cost would be relatively low—only 1 percent of GDP for the United States. Yet few countries today are on a path to reach even 80/50, and the United States actually increased its use of fossil fuels and carbon emissions in the years 2012 through 2014.

Rich countries must take the lead in developing carbon-free economies. So far, the European nations have been doing better than the United States. Germany is taking the lead by aiming for near-total renewable energy without nuclear energy by 2050, or a 100/50 goal. Although electric bills will increase slightly for German companies and residents, the transition to green energy will help economic growth because of the large investments in infrastructure. The German transition to clean energy, called *Energiewende*, is estimated to increase its GDP by 1 percent yearly, with a net increase in jobs from 2012 to 2030.

Climate experts now think that to keep global warming under the 2°C target, the 80 percent reduction in carbon emissions worldwide must be accomplished by 2030, not 2050. Rich countries must push for zero emissions as soon as possible. This may sound extreme, but research shows that 100 percent renewable energy by 2050 is possible using available technology for a reasonable social cost. The wind, water, and sunlight (WWS) roadmap from Stanford University shows how 139 countries can achieve an 80–85 percent conversion to WWS by 2030 and a 100 percent conversion by 2050. Similarly, the less ambitious Deep Decarbonization Pathways Project (DDPP), a collaborative global initiative spearheaded by the UN, shows how the 2°C limit can be accomplished in sixteen of the world's largest economies, including the United States, China, India, Japan, and Germany. The DDPP shows how the sixteen countries, which are responsible for three fourths of today's CO_2 emissions from energy, can reduce CO_2 emissions to 50 percent below 2010 by 2050, which is equivalent to reaching 75/50. The

DDPP targets are low, with the most ambitious target being 85/50. The less developed countries, especially China, would continue to increase CO_2 emissions until 2020, then slowly decrease them until 2030, when the decline becomes much steeper. India's low 2010 emissions would rise slightly until 2030 and then remain about the same until 2050. Even so, in 2050 India's emissions would be less than half of China's, and China's emissions would be as high as those of the other fifteen countries combined. The DDPP is a politically realistic start on the path to zero emissions.

We can do it!

Technology has played an important role, first in creating the carbon-based economy and today in creating a new carbon-free economy. Pricing fossil fuels correctly would unleash even more innovation and use the power of competition in a positive way. Once a technology is ready to be implemented broadly, competition can spur innovation and bring down the price. Solar panel modules, which use photovoltaic cells, are an excellent example of how once a market exists, the price falls rapidly and the technology improves. From 1979 to 2015, solar modules have fallen 22 percent in price for each doubling of volume. Between 2010 and 2014, module prices fell 20 to 30 percent.

A top technological priority today is to develop better energy-storage capabilities. At the consumer level, we need batteries for electric vehicles that are cheaper, longer-lasting, faster-charging, and lighter. At the community level, we need a way for public utilities to store energy during those times when the wind is not blowing, the sun is not shining, and the rivers are not turning hydroelectric turbines. The private sector is making excellent headway on electric car batteries, and governments are working to develop and implement energy storage capabilities for utilities.

Unfortunately, government subsidies to research and develop new technologies such as carbon capture and storage (CCS) do not always bring about the expected results. As we discussed earlier, the massive investments in CCS have yet to pay off, primarily because of their high cost compared to the low cost of fossil fuels. Governments have funded billions for CCS projects over the past decade, but using it at power stations is expensive and tricky.

Although nuclear energy is controversial because of past disasters in Russia, the United States, and Japan, many climate scientists think that the Generation 4 nuclear energy methods now being developed can be a safe and effective way to meet global energy needs. Six versions of Gen 4 are currently under development, and all offer advances in sustainability, costs, and safety. Fast reactors, in particular, reuse the spent uranium from Generation 3 plants, do not create nuclear waste, and are proliferation resistant (minimize the risk of weapons-grade nuclear material being stolen by terrorists or rogue nations). While this research is valuable in the long term, the serious drawback in nuclear energy is that a Gen 4 nuclear plant will take two to four decades to develop and then build, even if its proposed construction goes through unopposed. This is too long to wait to reach our 80/30 goal, especially when we already have the required technology to provide clean energy from solar, wind, and hydropower. However, the developing countries, especially China and India, with their billions of people needing more energy to live comfortable lives, could benefit from Gen 4 nuclear energy plants that are built after 2030, when these two countries are projected to be emitting a high seven gigatons of CO_2 in 2050 in the DDPP projections, or 70 percent of the total emissions of the 16 DDPP countries in 2050.

Share Green Technology to Create Prosperity Around the World

Rich industrialized countries created global warming with their carbon-based industrialization and growth. They now have the resources and the obligation to help poor countries obtain a sustainable growth path. One way is to provide their clean energy technology to developing countries to help improve their standard of living based on a sustainable economy. Countries rich and poor must integrate policies that mitigate global warming and reduce inequality, because these two crises have become intertwined.

Nonrich nations, including populous China and India, need economic growth in order to provide basic goods, health care, and education to all their citizens. These countries also need access to green technology and funding that supports sustainable economic growth so they can leapfrog over fossil fuel technologies to use only renewable energy.

One step toward reaching this goal is for industrialized countries to fulfill their pledge to raise $100 billion yearly through 2025 to help developing countries finance their transition to renewable energy and resilient adaptation to climate change. But the OECD reports that rich countries channeled the substantially lower amount of $61.8 billion to developing countries in 2014.

China and India show different examples of how emerging

economies respond to the climate crisis. China's fast growth has been based largely on coal, which has created unbearable air pollution. But in 2014, China committed to halting the expansion of its use of coal and expanding its use of natural gas, wind, and solar. In contrast, India, whose $5,701 GDP per person lags considerably behind China's $13,206 GDP per person, is focused on quickly growing its use of fossil fuels, especially cheap coal. India's expansion of its renewable energy efforts is far outweighed by its new investments in coal-fired plants, and now India is suffering from the world's most polluted air.

Overall, the OECD nations are decoupling their fossil fuel energy use from economic growth. But Buddhist economics wants them to push further in creating sustainable lifestyles that reduce wasteful consumption and reduce overwork so people have time to enjoy life and help one another. The industrialized countries have an obligation to transition rapidly to post-carbon economies and to redistribute consumption from the wealthy to the less well off, so that their total personal consumption does not grow. Then economic growth in industrialized countries will be based on spending to build the infrastructure for a modern post-carbon economy.

Part of the progress toward an improved standard of living in poorer countries will come from reducing birthrates in order to have zero or negative population growth, as has already been accomplished in nineteen European countries and Japan. The high birthrates in Southern Asia and Africa are a strain on the health of mothers and imperil a family's ability to feed its children. Providing health care and birth control to women around the world would give them necessary control over their lives and the chance to raise healthy and educated children. Plus without a growing population, a poor country is much better situated to provide all families with basic consumption and health care, and to educate their children, while making the transition to a sustainable economy.

The Tax and Transfer step in Buddhist economics tackles global warming, one of the four ecosystems being threatened by human activities. The next step, Sustainable Agriculture, involves the three other ecosystems currently under threat: the phosphorus-nitrogen cycle that makes agriculture possible; the land system, with its forests and freshwater sources; and biodiversity, or ensuring that species survive.

2. SUSTAINABLE AGRICULTURE

Industrial agriculture is responsible for emitting up to one third of global greenhouse gases, and its overuse of water and fertilizers devastates rivers, lakes, and oceans. Forests are cut down in order to graze livestock and grow soybeans for feed. Livestock and poultry consume more than 70 percent of soybeans worldwide. Deforestation causes loss of species and changes the weather, which causes droughts.

Industrial agriculture for livestock, along with the cultivation of palm oil, which is widely used in processed foods, has destroyed critical ecosystems in the rain forests of South America, Southern Asia, and Africa. Rain forests play an important role in local and global weather through their absorption and creation of rainfall and their absorption of carbon dioxide. Tropical forests create rain clouds, even far away from the forests. In addition, for many forest-rich developing countries, deforestation is the major source of their emissions pollution. If tropical forests were aggregated into a country, deforestation would rank above the European Union as a source of annual greenhouse gas emissions. Halting deforestation is a giant step that we must take if we are to temper climate change. To do this, rich countries must understand how our eating meat and palm oil results in poor countries' cutting down forests.

All countries must stop cutting down forests and replant pastures with native trees. People around the world are already planting some trees, and nations can take this one step further and plant and replant forests. The mantra should change from "Plant a tree" to "Plant a forest."

Sustainable agriculture practices that use land and water wisely include using compost and crop rotation to replenish the soil, using only natural pesticides, and raising animals humanely, without the use of hormones and daily antibiotics. These sustainable practices naturally replenish the earth, and they support bees and other species that are part of land ecosystems.

When industrialized countries finance sustainable agriculture programs in poorer countries, they must be mindful that the sustainability of rural communities is dependent on the health of their ecosystems and on their culture. Development projects need to focus on the holistic performance of the ecosystem rather than on the productivity of one development project, so that the resilience of the rural ecosystems remain intact to support the community's livelihood and culture.

A critical problem globally is how to supply the fresh water required by animals (including humans) and agriculture. The amount of water required grows with increases in global population and incomes, and the amount available declines with global warming. The production of meat, especially beef, uses a great deal of water. Today, as climate change melts glaciers and ice caps and worsens droughts, the damaged river systems are struggling to survive. Surface water from rivers, streams, and lakes is drying up, and we are extracting more and more groundwater and digging ever deeper into the ground.

Many people around the world do not have easy access to clean water, and some women and girls spend many hours a day carrying jugs of water from streams and lakes to their homes. People drinking contaminated water suffer from water-related diseases, including worms, diarrhea, and typhoid. Technologies to create potable water at a low cost are available at the community level or at the kitchen level for rural families, and several of these technologies are now being used in Africa and India. Researchers at my own university have developed technologies to provide inexpensive potable water. However, this is not enough—governments around the world must ensure universal and easy access to clean water; this is the UN's Sustainable Development Goal 6.

Countries vary enormously in their use of water per person. The amount reflects how agribusiness grows food, how much meat people eat, how lawns and gardens are maintained, and how wastefully people use water. Rich countries use much more water per person than poor countries. Americans use almost four times as much water as the Chinese, and twenty-two times as much as Nigerians. The United States even uses three times as much water as France, another advanced country where agriculture is powerful and profitable.

The world can do a much better job utilizing its precious clean water. Agriculture, industry, and cities withdraw three times more water than is actually consumed. The rest is released back into the system, often polluted, or is wasted. Agriculture wastes water by overwatering, inefficient irrigation, and letting water filled with pesticides and fertilizer flow back into rivers, seas, and oceans. New technologies to manage the watering of crops with the use of sensors have recently been developed, and they allow application of water to plants or trees only as needed, which can dramatically reduce water waste. Water conservation through better planning and management is essential to satisfying global water demands.

Hunger is also a global tragedy, with many children stunted by malnutrition and starvation. Developing sustainable agricultural around the world and regulating fishing can increase the food supply close to where people consume it and go a long way toward feeding the hungry. Rich countries can, and must, play an important role in implementing sustainable agriculture and regulating fishing both at home and abroad.

Another, and surely the simplest, way to make sure no one goes to bed hungry is to reduce waste. The United Nations reports that more than one third of the food produced is never consumed. Globally, 50 billion pounds (22.7 billion kilograms) of food is wasted each week, which is more than enough to feed the 800 million hungry people. Rich countries must stop wasting their overabundance of food, and all countries need to improve their food production to reduce waste. Food losses occur during the harvest, transport, and processing stages, both in poor and rich countries. In rich countries, food waste also occurs when stores and families toss out food, usually because of a single blemish or because too much food was purchased. The water and land used, and the greenhouse gas emitted, by food waste critically damages ecosystems. If food waste were a country, it would be the third-largest emitter of greenhouse gases in the world, right behind the United States and China—a stunning, immoral, and needless cost.

While children in extremely poor regions are stunted from malnutrition, children in nonpoor countries are suffering from health problems related to obesity. In the United States, where 17 percent of children and 35 percent of adults are obese, the Centers for Disease Control and Prevention declared, "The epidemic of obesity poses a grave threat to the health of the people of the United States." Consumption of soft drinks is a major source of sugary calories, especially for teens, yet attempts to tax soft drinks at the local and federal levels are fought by the beverage companies. For example, in my home-town of Richmond, California, with a hundred thousand residents, about half of the children are overweight or obese. A sugar tax was put on the Richmond city ballot in 2012. Big beverage companies poured $2.5 million into a campaign to convince small store owners and the voters that the tax was unfair and would raise prices. Soft drink companies won.

Local and national governments can regulate unhealthy foods with taxes, restrictions on sales in schools, and disclosure of information. If people's diets are causing health problems, the government must take action to protect public health.

3. MEASURE AND TRANSFORM

How do nations know if their economies are becoming more sustainable and equitable? By measuring economic performance. The GDP has been the yardstick for that measurement for

decades, but today, many economists and political leaders agree
that we must move beyond the GDP and find a broader measure
of well-being.

As discussed in Chapter 6, we can use a single-value measure
to track economic progress within a country and across countries,
and supplement it with a dashboard of indices for specific goals.
Both the measure of economic performance and the measure of
specific goals can incorporate the well-being of future generations
of our species as well as other species, who have no voice and rely
upon us to care about their well-being and act on their behalf.

The United Nations is the global leader in promoting sustainability and alleviating poverty. The UN has decades of experience in collecting and analyzing data and in bringing countries
together to work on sustainable development and climate
change. With a deep knowledge of these subjects, coupled with
the specific knowledge of its 193 members, the United Nations
is uniquely qualified to develop and implement a single-value
economic performance measure, such as the Genuine Progress
Indicator, for all countries, along with a complementary dashboard of specific indicators. Let's call this hypothetical single-
value performance measure the UN-GPI.

The UN-GPI would bring together three measurement
efforts: the UN's Human Development Index (HDI), along
with its adjustments for inequality and women's rights; the
UN's Sustainable Development Goals Index (SDGI), both the
aggregated index and the dashboard; and the UN's System of
Environmental-Economic Accounting (SEEA), which presents
a wide range of statistics and indicators regarding the earth's
energy, water, land resources, and ecosystems.

Together, these measures, along with data from the OECD

Better Life Index and other measures already being done around the world, can provide the inputs into the UN-GPI components, which are then aggregated into one value to track economic performance. This effort will require partnerships with other global organizations, such as the World Bank, the IMF, and the OECD. The World Bank has already set up a partnership group, Wealth Accounting and Valuation of Ecosystem Services (WAVES), to help countries and companies implement natural capital accounting based on the SEEA.

The strengths of the UN-GPI single-value measure are its breadth and its ability to encompass economic performance in both industrialized and developing countries. Economic performance grows in richer countries when they transfer status consumption by the wealthy to basic consumption by the poor; when they reduce the workweek to allow time for family and community activities; and when they reduce wasteful spending. The economic performance of poorer countries grows when basic consumption, education, and health care for everyone improve. All countries show better performance when their depletion of natural capital goes down and their ecosystems are healing.

The supplementary dashboard indicators used in conjunction with the UN-GPI can show important nonmarket indices, such as the Cantril Ladder that measures people's life satisfaction (happiness). The dashboard could also include data that measure how well countries are doing on specific goals. For example, the Sustainable Development Goals dashboard is an important step forward in measuring how well countries are doing in the areas of human rights, human opportunities, security, and other hard-to-measure aspects of quality of life that are not incorporated into the single-value measure, UN-GPI.

Yes, sensible, well-meaning people disagree on what matters to people and to countries, and even on what the relevant economic goals are. Some experts argue against aggregating indicators into a single-value measure, but I argue that the potential for learning from it is worth the problems. The UN knows how to compromise to get a job done and move forward. We can learn as we go along, and the single-value measure and the dashboard can be expanded and improved upon with experience.

In fact, without a single-value measure of quality of life, I fear that rich countries will continue to feast on consumption rather than make the transition to a sustainable world where life is based on meaningful relations and activities in harmony with Nature. A critical part of the transformation process lies in changing our thinking, habits, and daily activities. People's ideas of what constitutes a good life evolve as they achieve a comfortable lifestyle and realize that happiness depends more on health, good relationships, security, and helping others than it does on wealth. Chasing after money brings pain instead of happiness. Measuring economic performance as quality of life rather than GDP changes the conversation, and it helps both countries and people focus on creating meaningful lives for everyone. It is a key step toward implementing Buddhist economics.

4. PEACE AND PROSPERITY

Human well-being is currently being threatened by war and violence on a massive scale, with civil wars raging in multiple nations, other wars being waged by powerful countries led by the United States and Russia, and vicious acts of terrorism occurring worldwide. The ongoing Syrian refugee crisis in

Europe is only one of the latest human tragedies caused by war and violence.

The United States and its allies have been engaged in their war on terrorism for fifteen years now. The outcome seems to be the creation of more terrorism, violence, and hatred. Buddhist economics suggests another approach: replace war with humanitarian aid and long-term support for political, economic, and social progress.

This approach echoes that of the Economists for Peace and Security: "to promote non-military solutions to world challenges, and more broadly to work towards freedom from fear and want for all." Their motto is a Somali proverb: "War and famine. Peace and milk." Their excellent research by world-renowned scholars has taught me about the economics of war and peace.

One critical way to help end violence is to restrict the extremely profitable global arms trade. The ability to buy arms easily has supported civil wars and terrorism worldwide and has resulted in yet more political repression, human rights abuses, and untold deaths and human suffering.

The global arms trade declined from a high level in the early 1980s until the early 2000s, when it began to expand again. The five largest exporters of weapons from 2010 to 2014 were the United States (31%) and Russia (27%), followed by China, Germany, and France (5% each). Together, these five nations accounted for about 75 percent of all weapons sold.

The six largest importers of weapons from 2010 to 2014 were India (15%), followed by Saudi Arabia and China (5% each), and the UAE, Pakistan, and Australia (4% each). The global trade in weapons fluctuates from country to country as it reflects the wars being fought. In 2014, Saudi Arabia dramatically increased its weapons imports, replacing India as the world's largest weapons importer.

In the noble attempt to restrain traded arms from being used in conflicts and the repression of human rights, the United Nations negotiated the landmark Arms Trade Treaty (ATT) in 2014; it covers all conventional arms, from small arms to warships. Seventy-seven countries agreed to assess the risk that arms sales would be used in conflicts or cause human rights abuse, and to halt transfers of arms across their borders when the risk became extremely high. The treaty also bans arms transfers that violate a UN arms embargo. Significantly, Russia and China did not sign the ATT, though other top exporters, including the United States, Germany, and France, did. Of the top six importers of weapons, only Australia and the United Arab Emirates signed the treaty.

No single nation can ensure world peace. Only a concerted global effort (led, for example, by the United Nations) combined with regional negotiations for specific conflicts, can pave the way to implementing nonmilitary solutions to conflicts and repression. However, national governments are responsible for what happens at home. Only national governments can ensure basic human rights for all people within their borders, stamp out internal corruption and violence, and instill trust in all levels of government.

So far, Buddhist economics has been mostly silent on the role that companies play in the economy. The free market model mandates that corporations maximize profits and minimize any other goal that reduces profits. Adhering to the free market model, big business usually fights against policies that are cornerstones of Buddhist economics, such as a higher minimum or living wage, progressive taxation, restrictions on pollution, regulation of work hours, and paid family leave. Big business has used its resources to lobby against policies such as these, and to lobby for subsidies and regulations that increase their power and profits. Meanwhile, small and medium-sized companies have ended up riding on the coattails of big business.

And yet, large companies vary enormously in how they treat workers and in how their operations and products impact the world. Many have signed on to "corporate social responsibility" or "green initiatives" to improve their ways, as well as their profits. Some of these initiatives have had a positive impact, while others have been implemented cynically, for marketing purposes. The derogatory term "greenwash" tags a company for bragging about its environmentally friendly products while it simultaneously degrades the environment on a massive scale.

To find companies that treat all stakeholders well—workers, society, and the environment—we have to search hard. But there are a few, such as Working Assets (now Credo) in the United States, which was founded in 1985 to provide credit card and phone services with the aim of donating a portion of their revenue to social causes. To date, over $80 million has been donated to nonprofit organizations, especially those supporting human rights and environmental justice. Another example is Interface, from the petroleum-intensive manufacturing carpet industry. The company made a major change in direction in 1994, "from a plunderer of the earth to an agent of its restoration." They redesigned their production process and products to use new technologies and systems that used renewable materials and energy and reduced waste and harmful emissions.

Other bright spots are social enterprises—small companies with missions to solve a major problem or impact a social goal. These can be for-profit or nonprofit, and they operate mostly in developing regions to provide jobs and services to people, often through using new technologies or innovative approaches. I have worked with graduate students at Berkeley who developed and deployed new technologies to improve the standard of living in poorer regions, especially Africa and India. Every major business school has a social entrepreneurship program, and you as an individual can support social enterprises—look for them locally or online.

Big companies do have a role to play in creating an equitable, sustainable world. The next two steps focus on how companies can do their part in taking the leap to Buddhist economics. The first step concerns how larger companies or organizations can move toward being more equitable and sustainable, both internally (along their supply chain) and externally (with their products and services). The second step focuses on how companies can help create a Buddhist economy by paying their workers living wages with work hours that provide time to live meaningful lives.

5. GREEN PRODUCTION AND GREEN PRODUCTS

Companies around the world can change the way they operate to reduce their environmental impact and carbon footprint. A company's investments in retooling for carbon-free operations can greatly reduce greenhouse gas emissions while preserving

rofits. A Harvard Business School study found that
ı-sustainability companies outperformed compa-
stainability companies in the stock market over the
period from 1993 to 2009. Yet overall, business has been slow to
adopt sustainability procedures.

The companies that face the biggest risk to their bottom
line, as fossil fuel reserves are devalued, are the fossil fuel corporations themselves, plus automobile manufacturers, industrial
agriculture, and other industries that are big fossil fuel energy
users. Because they have so much to gain, these industries are a
prime place in which to push for carbon-free restructuring.

With climate change, risk management is becoming an ever-
larger problem for all companies, which must figure out how
climate change, energy prices, and reduced carbon pollution
will impact their profits over the years. When companies are
ready to integrate environmental sustainability across operations and products, however, they don't have to look very far
for information and tool kits to help them manage energy and
water use better.

The companies that provide insurance to big business face
enormous risk. Mark Carney, the governor of the Bank of
England, warned the insurance industry that climate change
affects a nation's financial stability through "physical risks, such
as claims from floods and storms; liability risks that could arise
if those suffering climate change losses sought compensation
from those they held responsible; and transition risks caused by
the revaluation of assets [fossil fuel deposits] caused by the
adjustment to a lower-carbon economy."

Another study done at the London School of Economics estimates that without action to reduce GHG emissions, climate

change could decrease the value of global financial assets by $2.5 trillion by the end of this century, but in the worst-case scenario, the losses could soar to $24 trillion, or 17 percent of the world's financial assets. Reducing emissions to stay under the 2°C target cuts these losses by one third to one half.

Much of the insurance industry understands that companies have billions to lose. Large insurers are pushing client companies and governments to plan and act now to make the transition to a resilient, carbon-free world. The private sector has responded. The UK-based nonprofit CDP collects and makes public the environmental impact data from global companies and reports on the link between management practices to mitigate climate change and profitability. In partnership with the Climate Group, CDP launched a global initiative called RE100, made up of more than fifty major companies in Europe, the United States, China, and India that have pledged to use 100 percent renewable energy by dates they specify. The White House brought together more than eighty large multinational companies to sign a pledge to tackle climate change and to support the commitments made at COP21 in Paris. The companies describe what they are doing, and they set their own targets or goals.

A plenitude of sources exist for companies that want to be guided by Buddhist economics. One longtime leader in this area is European economist Laszlo Zsolnai. His books provide a way to learn about how companies, in collaboration with their stakeholders, can operate in a humanistic, sustainable way that respects ecological and social constraints. Another excellent source for holistic company management are the books by U.S. economist Chris Laszlo. He is a leader in teaching how businesses can use advances in sustainable design for optimal social and environmental performance.

Corporate social responsibility (CSR), an older add-on to the mainstream business model, is one approach that companies have used in the past to help solve social problems as they improve their impact on workers, customers, shareholders, communities, and the world. Now in use for over half a century, CSR provides a long list of ways in which corporations can behave more responsibly. A wide array of studies on the impact of CSR on corporate profits and reputations show mixed results, at best.

With today's focus on stopping global warming and rebuilding threatened ecosystems, though, CSR does not provide the tools that twenty-first-century companies need to manage risk in the transition to a carbon-free world. A more realistic, yet challenging, approach to sustainable production is "circular production," which simultaneously reduces waste, uses renewable energy, and supports the environment. The idea is that all production should use renewable resources and all consumption should be recycled back into the system to be reused. Manufacturers redesign products to be ecologically friendly and nonpolluting, and these products go on to become part of the natural cycle of environmental regeneration.

Although scholars and activists have suggested many ways for companies to be socially responsible and operate sustainably, few companies have acted on them. Without having to pay directly for environmental degradation until they are sued, and with governments slow to regulate even unwise uses of energy, companies remain free to pursue high profits without worrying about environmental degradation. Big business needs the guiding hand of government regulation and taxes to take the ethical, sustainable path.

As the net returns from incorporating environmental, social, and governance (ESG) factors into private investment decisions become clearer, the private sector will play a bigger role. The UN Environment Programme Finance Initiative has worked with more than two hundred banking, insurance, and investment organizations to analyze the relationship between ESG factors and financial performance, in order to promote six principles for responsible investment. An example of this effort is an investment consortium of long-term investors whose goal is to identify and invest in ESG-conscious companies and projects.

Companies also need to be pushed by customers and society to stop polluting the environment and to use carbon-free energy. One way to put pressure on fossil-fuel-dependent industries is through divesting from their stock. Today's divestment movement began on college campuses and has spread across the United States and Europe to churches and civic organizations. Organizations with large pension and endowment funds can play a big role in pushing fossil-fuel-related industries to leave carbon in the ground and move to renewable energy through divestment.

Unfortunately, though, many organizations have bought into the hoax pushed by the natural gas industry, that natural gas is a clean and necessary bridge from coal to renewable energy. The University of California, where I teach, and Stanford have divested from both coal and tar sands stocks, but not from other fossil-fuel-related stocks. They have taken a helpful first step, but it is not enough.

Through regulation, carbon taxes, and public action, we can push fossil fuel companies to become clean energy companies and leave their fossil fuel reserves in the ground.

6. LIVING WAGES AND A BALANCED LIFE

The transition to creating sustainable, meaningful lives for all people must include a discussion about jobs. Everyone needs a job that does not destroy their humanity, that pays a living wage for a comfortable sustainable lifestyle, and that allows time for family and community activities. Jobs that pay slave wages, or leave workers depleted, or require hours of overwork are not compatible with happiness. To achieve this, we need government policies that enforce minimum wages, overtime pay, and paid leave for family care.

Full disclosure: labor economics is my field, and I have spent many years studying and teaching labor markets. Among the subjects I have examined are employment, earnings, benefits, discrimination, unemployment, and the standard of living. Buddhist economists say companies can leap ahead by:

- Reducing the exorbitant pay of CEOs and other executives;
- Increasing the pay of workers so everyone makes a living wage; and
- Reducing the working hours of all workers, not just those covered by overtime pay.

We already mentioned research showing that at large firms, the CEO's pay is not related to their value-added or to the company's performance. Worse yet, the earnings gap between executives and other earners reflects corporate power. As worker power has plummeted in the past forty years, the wage gap between the wealthy executive and all other workers has grown to produce historic inequality.

To restore morale and equity, companies must restructure the earnings schedule to shift earnings from the very top 0.1 percent to workers in the bottom 40 percent and bring the earnings gap back to a reasonable level. An MIT study turned heads in 2014 when it showed that companies using human-centered strategies that provide good jobs with a living wage and empowerment at work have superior performance.

We already mentioned other policies that support living wages, such as increasing workers' bargaining power, raising the minimum wage, and prohibiting imports produced with substandard labor practices, such as child and slave labor or long work days or unsafe conditions.

More paid time off and flexible family leave policies are compatible with profitability, as we already observed in Northern European, French, and German companies. However, these countries can go further in shortening the workweek in addition to providing paid time off through vacation time. Overworked employees become burned out and develop health problems. Overworking with meager vacation time, as seen in the United States and Japan, should not be the professional way of life.

Buddhist economics calls on nations and the business community to lead the way in creating a sustainable economy with shared prosperity. Companies can do so by turning to the research publications and organizations listed in this book for guidance and support. Now is the time for companies to join governments and the people to stop destroying the ecosystems and create quality of life for all.

Each of us can also leap forward to a Buddhist economy on a personal level. Below are two steps for individuals to take, first in their own lives and then in concert with others.

7. LIVE MINDFULLY WITH LOVE, COMPASSION, AND WISDOM

Each of us can play a part in creating meaningful, happy lives for ourselves and our communities. The guidelines are:

- live mindfully with love and compassion
- care for others and relieve suffering
- enjoy and rejuvenate the earth

These guidelines may be simple, but following them in daily life is challenging. We are surrounded by a materialistic culture that pushes us to buy this, buy that. Money demands and social roles create endless claims on our time that can never be fully satisfied. We feel overwhelmed, frustrated, and inadequate to the demands of life much of the time.

Buddhist economics says:

Stop. Sit quietly and appreciate the wonders of the moment. Breathe, and think about all the good parts of your life—the outing you took with family or friends last weekend, the good food you ate today, the lovely tree outside the window, the sick friend you helped, the charity you support. Be grateful for the people who enrich your life, and for the earth that supports you. Let go of your ego, which defines reality by your mental projections and rules daily life by mental habits. Listen to your Buddha nature of love and compassion.

Sitting quietly and savoring the moment is an important way to begin practicing a mindful and meaningful life.

The Buddhist Declaration on Climate Change reminds us: "Both as individuals and as a species, we suffer from a sense of self that feels disconnected not only from other people but from the Earth itself. As Thich Nhat Hanh has said, 'We are here to awaken from the illusion of our separateness.' We need to wake up and realize that the Earth is our mother as well as our home—and in this case the umbilical cord binding us to her cannot be severed. When the Earth becomes sick, we become sick, because we are part of her."

Remember that we are interdependent with one another. Don't confuse being hyperconnected on social media with being interconnected in human spirit. Put your iPhone down. Look for ways to connect with the people around you—family, friends, strangers. When you are feeling unhappy because of all the demands on your life, help someone you know. Think about what is important to you, what you really care about, what makes life meaningful. Let the other things fall off your to-do list.

Replace shopping trips with spending more time with family or helping friends. When you are shopping, before buying another gadget or more shoes, ask: Do I need this?

Practice living simply, which frees up time to spend in activities that bring you joy: hanging out with friends, playing with your kids, writing in your journal, creating art, working in the garden, cooking what you bought at the farmers' market.

Enjoying life isn't about how you spend your money; it is about how you spend your time.

For many people, creating a meaningful life requires that they work fewer hours and balance their work and family activities and obligations. This takes serious thought and brainstorming with people at work and at home. Focus on well-being rather than income. Figure out how much control you have over your work hours and how much you want or need to work. As we spend less time at work, we can spend more time caring for others, helping our communities, working in the garden and on home projects, and being creative, as well as hanging out with friends and enjoying life.

We are all part of the earth, yet our human activities are irreparably damaging the earth. An important part of living mindfully in harmony with Nature is learning how our activities harm the ecosystems and other people. You may have already calculated your carbon and water footprints, and you may already be changing your daily actions to support the earth. Yet many of us are slow to shrink our large carbon footprint. We justify our actions because we are well intentioned and are helping others through our work and other activities. Our time is valuable, and we are already overloaded with all the things we must do.

This used to be my own frame of mind, until I watched the documentary *An Inconvenient Truth* in 2006. I calculated my carbon footprint online and was patting myself on the back as I plowed through the questions with green answers. Suddenly I was taken up short when I tallied up my air travel. I had been traveling around the United States and Japan studying the semiconductor industry, and air travel made my carbon footprint astonishingly and embarrassingly large. I brainstormed with my research team on how we could fly less to accomplish our field-work, and we began doing some interviews on Skype rather than in person. I fly as little as possible now and use Internet and mobile connections for work meetings as well as for staying in touch with faraway family and friends.

Here are some of the ways in which my family has lowered our carbon emissions: We drive less and lease a small electric car, driving our older Prius only on longer trips. We recycle all paper, plastic, and cans. We compost, have a worm farm, and use only natural pesticides (insecticidal soap and Neem oil) in the garden. Our trash can for the landfill has almost nothing in it. I wear a wetsuit instead of sunscreen in the oceans (sunscreen kills coral). We replaced our small lawn with native plants. My husband continually weatherizes our place.

When it's chilly, we put on more clothes or grab a lap blanket and keep the thermostat set on a cooler temperature. When it's hot, we create a breeze by opening windows or using a small fan before turning on the air conditioner. We open car windows when driving around town and run the car AC as little as possible, and then at 72 degrees. When home from work or seeing friends, we don "around the house" clothes in order to do less laundry and dry cleaning. We collect "gray" water from the shower and the kitchen sink to water plants in pots outside the door. We run the dishwasher infrequently. We wrap presents with comics or calendar pages or whatever paper we've saved.

In my daily life, Buddhist economics guides me to be mindful in eating as well as in responding to external events, with the saying *Don't have a cow!* This translates literally to *Don't eat beef* (or lamb), and figuratively, *Relax*.

Not eating beef or lamb is a big step in helping the earth. The carbon and water footprints of beef and lamb are much larger than those of other animals (see Chapter 4). My family eats other animal products sparingly (or none at all). Plus we eat all the food we purchase, with the scraps going to the worms, and we shop at the local farmers market.

As I go through the day, I often pause and repeat the Buddhist prayer, "May we heal Mother Earth as we heal ourselves." This puts me in touch with myself and my surroundings, as it reminds me to support the environment and reduce suffering whenever I can.

You can add to the list as you move from a closetful to a mindful way of life. We don't want to harm the earth, and we want to reduce suffering around the world as we enjoy life and support the earth.

8. WORK TOGETHER AND TAKE ACTION

Thich Nhat Hanh teaches us, "The healing of our bodies and minds must go together with the healing of the Earth . . . Together, we can bring about real transformation for ourselves and for the world . . . We will survive and thrive together with our Mother Earth, or we will not survive at all."

We know that one person alone cannot make much difference, but we know that together, we can do much. Rallies around the world before the Paris 2015 climate change conference helped push governments into signing an agreement to keep global warming below 2°C. Post-Paris, environmental activists returned home to focus mostly on local issues, such as shutting down coal power plants, stopping new fossil fuel explorations in public lands, stopping the fracking of natural gas in the United States, ending fuel exploration in the rain forests in Brazil, and ending open-pit coal mining in Germany.

One of my heroes is Bill McKibben, founder of 350.org. He tells us that when he feels discouraged about humans destroying our way of life on earth, he goes out to work on creating change with others. Campaigns and rallies can make a difference. President Obama rejected the Keystone Pipeline project on climate grounds after being confronted with a relentless and popular campaign against it for many months.

Environmental justice campaigns might be strictly local, or part of larger national campaigns, or even part of coordinated global campaigns led by groups such as Greenpeace or Friends of the Earth. In the United States and Canada, groups such as 350.org, the Environmental Defense Fund, the Nature Conservancy, and the Sierra Club use social media to organize campaigns at the local and state level. The Climate Action Network (CAN) coordinates almost a thousand of these climate action groups in worldwide events, such as the "Break Free" events around the world in May 2016 to demand a halt to fossil fuel operations and an accelerated transition to 100 percent renewable energy. A positive legacy of the climate crisis is that our collective response is building a more caring community, augmenting our citizenship roles with public action, and expanding our participation in, and donations to, environmental organizations and nonpolluting causes.

As we work together on climate change, we must be ready for the backlash from the wealthy fossil fuel energy companies and the organizations and politicians they fund. Big Oil will fight to block regulations to reduce the use of coal, oil, and gas.

We already observe how they spend millions of dollars to fight against demands to reduce carbon emissions, and how they spread lies and misleading information to confuse people (and voters) about climate change and what causes it. Big Oil has the resources to restructure themselves as renewable energy companies. Instead they have decided to use their resources to fight "Keep it in the ground," with minor investments in renewable energy. They deny they are causing global warming and climate change. Unfortunately, too, the fossil fuel industry has successfully convinced many people that climate change is a hoax, or is unproven.

Exxon's own scientists had evidence as early as the 1970s that fossil fuels would warm the atmosphere to dangerous levels. In the following decades, Exxon hid this research, and then they joined with other fossil fuel companies and the foundations they support to deny that global warming was occurring and to raise doubts about the climate science research. The fossil fuel industry has followed the path taken by the tobacco companies, who were experts at hiding and then denying their own research showing tobacco is lethal to humans. Public outrage (see #exxonknew) helped push New York and Massachusetts to investigate whether Exxon violated the law by withholding the research on climate change, which harmed its shareholders.

In addition to addressing climate change, we also want to help our communities be sustainable and supportive places to live. A lot is happening at the local level that is worth supporting. Cities are building better public transit and are restructuring to make biking and walking safe and enjoyable alternatives to driving cars. Urban areas are setting up waste management systems so that people in high-density areas can recycle and compost as part of their daily habits. Cities are also helping businesses and residents make buildings more energy efficient. Rooftop gardens are sprouting up on top of buildings.

You can work with friends, neighbors, and organizations in a multitude of ways to reduce the suffering of people, especially elders and children. One area where volunteers make a difference is in providing support systems for seniors, both for those still living at home and for those who have moved into assisted living residences. We know that having a support system when you need help is vital to one's sense of well-being. Volunteers help elders go to the drugstore or doctor and take care of their mail, or just have a cup of tea with them, or say hello by phone. Another area in which volunteers make a difference is in working with students, perhaps as after-school tutors for struggling students, or as assistant coaches for sports teams, or as teachers' aides in the early grades. The volunteer and the elder or student build a relationship that enriches everyone.

As we change our lifestyles and expectations in a Buddhist economy, new habits and new values evolve. Together we can end the way big business rules the economy, the way the elite obtain wealth and use it to manipulate the system. The government resumes its role to ensure a fair and just economy that works for everyone. With a focus on well-being rather than income, we add to national well-being as together we reduce work hours and unemployment, restore natural capital and social capital, improve the distribution of resources, and have more time to care for others and enjoy life.

To embrace and practice Buddhist economics, you need courage. Courage to change, courage to protect the environment, courage to promote justice, and courage to live with joy.

At the personal level, you need courage to quit the rat race of overworking to make more money, courage to live mindfully as you help others, and courage to enjoy life off the treadmill. At the national level, you need courage to demand that your government provide the infrastructure needed for an economy that protects the environment and reduces carbon emissions, one that defines economic growth as improved well-being rather than more income. We also need the political will and courage to take action for ourselves on behalf of all species and future generations.

There is no end to a book on Buddhist economics, because it is a lifetime commitment and process. May we continue the journey together.

As social animals we need love and compassion.
These are the best human qualities.
With these we can take care of our society.

Dalai Lama, 2015

ACKNOWLEDGMENTS

I am grateful for the vision and support expressed by friends and strangers over the past five years that made this book a reality. In 2012 when psychology professor Christina Maslach listened to me talk about Buddhist economics over lunch, she suggested that I teach a sophomore seminar. The following spring 2013, my Buddhist Economics seminar began under the auspices of the UC Berkeley sophomore seminar program, which had been created by Maslach when she was vice provost. I am especially grateful to the undergraduates in the seminar, and to my graduate students over the years, for their creative and probing analyses that expanded my thinking.

I have learned from discussions and seminars with my faculty colleagues at Berkeley and beyond, especially Alice Agogino, George Akerlof, Bob Anderson, David Anthoff, Max Auffhammer, Pranab Bardhan, Eric Brewer, Jenna Burrell, David Card, Karen Chapple, Jack Colford, Stefano Dellavigna, Troy Duster, Barry Eichengreen, Marion Foucade, Gillian Hart, Arlie Hochschild, Dave Hodges, Herma Hill Kay, Dan Kammen, Dacher Keltner, George Lakoff, David Levine, Jim Lincoln, Joseph Lough, Mary Ann Mason, David Matza, Sanjyot

Mehendale, Dick Norgaard, Tappan Parikh, Jeff Perloff, Matthew Potts, Steve Raphael, Isha Ray, Michael Reich, Lee Riley, Steve Roach, Emmanuel Saez, Robert Sharf, Jesse Rothstein, AnnaLee Saxenian, Margaret Taylor, Laura Tyson, David Vogel, Kim Voss, Janet Yellen, Shelly Zedeck, Gabriel Zucman, and my mentor, the late Lloyd Ulman.

I am grateful to my close friends who provided helpful feedback on early drafts: Sanford Jacoby, Betsy Partridge, Pauline Sortor, Myra Strober, and Alison Taylor. At the end, when I could no longer re-read clearly, Daniel Matza-Brown came to my rescue with a careful, insightful reading.

I gratefully acknowledge the financial and administrative support from the Institute for Research on Labor and Employment (IRLE) at UC Berkeley for my research on measuring economic performance. IRLE has been my home away from home over the years, going back to when IRLE was IIR, the Institute for Industrial Relations. Countless discussions with Ken Jacobs, Katie Quan, Carol Zabin, and many others pushed my thinking. Andrew Chong, Eli Lazarus, and Maria Oldiges provided excellent research assistance and made original contributions.

My work on Buddhist economics evolved as key people became interested and spread the word. Kathleen Maclay's insightful article about my course in the *Berkeley News* put me in touch with scholars around the world. Then I drew upon spirited discussions with both old and new colleagues to make this book come alive. I am especially indebted to Rosemary Batt, Joanne and Kurt Bayer, Gunseli Berik, Sam Bowles, Tania Burchardt, Wendy Carlin, Dav Clark, Diana Coyle, Peter Coyote, Peter Daniels, Bill Easterly, Joe Engelberg, Robert Frank, Daniel

Goleman, Ian Gough, Ursula Huws, Mary Rose Kaczorowski, Kathy Ketchum, Nicola Lacey, Julia Lane, Jeff Madrick, Julie Matthaei, Bill McKibben, Dan Nixon, Phil Oreopoulis, Yong Paik, Achuthan Palat, Eleni Pallas, Thinlay Penjore, Thomas Piketty, Natalie Popovich, Andrew Ross, Gale Ryan, Paul Ryan, Jeffrey Sachs, Sonia Sachs, Amartya Sen, David Soskice, Kirsten Spalding, and Joe Stiglitz, Tim Sturgeon, and Laszlo Zsolnai. I am grateful to those who took time to teach me about the important work being done by their organizations: Glenn Everett at the UN-ONS; Pablo Freund on measuring national well-being; Pablo Freund at Buckminster Fuller Institute; Catherine Mann at the OECD; and Charles Seaford at the New Economics Foundation (UK).

Teresa Ghilarducci, Director of the Schwartz Center for Economic Policy Analysis at the New School, arranged two stimulating days for me to learn from a group of scholars whose view of the world mirrors Buddhist economics: Lopa Banerjee, Raphaele Chappe, Duncan Foley, David Howell, Rick McGahey, and Anwar Shaikh.

Harindra B. Dassanayake from the Presidential Secretariat of Sri Lanka invited me to work on sustainable development from a Buddhist perspective. During a memorable trip with my husband to Sri Lanka in February 2016, I learned from discussions with a wide array of people, including Harindra, Iraj De Alwis, Karin Fernando, Saman Kelegama, Mohan Muasinghe, Ven. Vajiraramaye Nanasiha, Arjuna Seneviratne, and Ven. Wimalarathana.

In India a special week of deep interactive discussion occurred at Sarnath International Nyingma Institute, where Director Tsering Gellek arranged for twenty learned monastics from India and Nepal to study global warming for two weeks with their teachers Andy Francis, Patricia Farland, and Todd Shaw in preparation for my visit. When I arrived, we studied climate science for two intense days, and then had a formal debate on the question foremost on my mind: "Can the Dharma help us solve global warming?" The careful, vigorous, and enlightening debate went on for four hours. Even though I was the judge of the debate, I am still learning from the experience. Two of the esteemed monks stand out in my mind, Khenpo Kunsang and Khenpo Dorje.

In Dharamsala, Tibetans Lhakpa Kyizom and Lobsang Tenzin ensured that we experienced both learning and enjoyment. On our visit to Center for Tibetan Authority (CTA), where the exiled Tibetan government resides, Naga Saugyas taught us about language and philosophy, and his tour vividly demonstrated the role of the CTA. We also thank Rohitash Jaikaria for showing us Hindu temples and tea gardens, and a bow to Deepak Gupta and Rakesh Gupta for making India special in the midst of air and noise pollution.

Trekking through Nepal and around sacred Mount Kailash, Tibet, in fall 2011, my thinking and well-being benefitted from long talks with Buddhist friends Linnea and Rick Christiani, Janet Ewing, and Bob Hoffman along with our leader, Joe Pilaar.

My gratitude to Anam Thubten Rinpoche for his teachings and wisdom, along with members of our sangha for sharing their knowledge and love: Sharon and Jeff Roe, Diane Schneider, Weegi and George Ryan, Ken White, Brooke Deterline, Paul Hawken, Sarah Laitinen, Jacob Archuletta, Tom Petersen, Laura Duggan, Deborah Henderson, Bing Budiarto, Catherine Hollander, Cynthia Barbaccia, Sandra Hansen, Kunzang

Roesler, and JB Colson. I was grateful for the opportunity to host Master Haebong and Kilung Rinpoche, who eagerly discussed climate change.

Buddhist teachers who are helping to heal Earth and stop global warming are especially important to me. They include Ayya Santussika and the Buddhist Climate Action Network, James Baraz and Scoop Nisker at Spirit Rock, and Khyentse Rinpoche. My own courage is bolstered by the Green Earth Sangha, with hugs to Nan Parks, Sean Munding, Sheila Tarbert, and Shine Garg. I was grateful for the opportunity to host Master Haebong and Kilung Rinpoche, who eagerly discussed climate change.

My meditation hut is my place of refuge, with gratitude to Tom Ratcliff, Andrew Butt, Humphrey Ratcliff, and Richard Katz for designing and building it in 2012.

The Richmond Art Center is my creative place of refuge, where I join with many talented and kind ceramic artists to build my clay sculptures with Buddhist and earth imagery. You can see them in our garden and perched on the fence, outside of my hut.

I fondly remember my two-week residency at the Mesa Refuge, where I completed my manuscript while watching Earth's beauty and enjoying the inquisitive minds and kindness of other writers, especially Peter Barnes and Susan Tillet, Christian McEwen and Nicole Perlroth.

Working with other environmental activists has given me courage to work tirelessly to stop global warming. Thank goodness for 350 East Bay, whose activists share their political savvy and energy, especially Amy Allen, Kathy Dervin, Jack Fleck, Richard Gray, Ken Jones, Judy Pope, and Carla West. Together we will "Keep it in the ground."

My neighbors keep my spirits high and make life fun, especially Sandra and Bruce Beyaert, Michael Couzens and Adi Givens, Ilza and Don Lewis, Lesli Handmacher, Carol and Roger Craine, Kate Harps and Dale Roberts, Donna Stoneham and Julie Nestingen, Steve Schaffran, Judy Canfield, and Karen and Andy Fisher. Farther away, I still feel the support of my close friends Melissa Appleyard, Peter Rappoport and Marcia Marley, and Diane and Phil Brumder.

My sons, Daniel and Jason, have enriched my life, and helped me find the path to live mindfully with loving kindness and joy. Grandsons, Max and Timmy, and their mom, Maura, keep me in touch with my Buddha nature, and teach me time and again to enjoy each precious moment. With gratitude to my brother Norman, my sister Eileen, Taylor and Jaja, and the Vermont (and beyond) Katz relatives for all their love and glorious living.

The reader may want to join me in thanking my Garamond agent, Lisa Adams, and my Bloomsbury editor, Nancy Miller. In complementary roles, their early vision brought the book into being, and their talent, hard work, and patience made the book readable. The Bloomsbury team has been terrific: George Gibson, Sara Kitchen, Cristina Gilbert, Marie Coolman, and Laura Keefe.

Eternal gratitude to my husband, Richard Katz, who has always been by my side to share the Buddhist journey, to lift me up when feeling down, and to provide the right word.

For everyone I forgot to thank, know that your contribution is not forgotten as we are all interconnected.

My thanks to you for reading this book. May we heal Mother Earth as we heal ourselves, for the benefit of all.

NOTES

Introduction

x   The Dalai Lama tells us: Dalai Lama, *The Art of Happiness, 10th Anniversary Edition: A Handbook for Living* (New York: Riverhead, 2009), 95.

xii   The *New York Times* article reported: Christopher F. Schuetze, "Superyachts to the Rescue," *New York Times*, January 16, 2015.

xii   inequality has dramatically increased: Anthony Atkinson, Thomas Piketty, and Emmanuel Saez, "Top Incomes in the Long Run of History," *Journal of Economic Literature* 49 (1), 2011, 3–71, series maintained in the World Top Incomes Database, http://topincomes. parisschoolofeconomics.eu/.

xii   Economists have warned us: Atkinson et al., JEL (2011); Stiglitz (2012); Frank (2007).

xii   ordinary people paid the price: Oxfam International, "Wealth: Having it All and Wanting More," January 2015.

xii   Income inequality is not uniform: Anthony B. Atkinson, Thomas Piketty, and Emmanuel Saez, "Top Incomes in the Long Run of History," *Journal of Economic Literature* 49 (2011): 3–71. doi: 10.1257/jel.49.1.3.

xiv   the Dalai Lama's belief: Dalai Lama, *The Art of Happiness, 10th Anniversary Edition: A Handbook for Living* (New York: Riverhead, 2009), 54.

xiv   "Every religion emphasize[s] human improvement": http://www .spiritualityandpractice.com/books/excerpts.php?id=16195.

xiv   achieve lasting happiness: Dalai Lama, *Ethics for the New Millennium* (New York: Riverhead, 1999), 20.

xvii a Harvard Medical School newsletter: The Harvard Medical School HEALTHbeat email newsletter of June 14, 2014, provides a mindfulness meditation exercise in four steps and has a booklet: *Positive Psychology: Harnessing the Power of Happiness, Mindfulness, and Inner Strength.*

xvii shown to increase brain activity: Berkeley Wellness online, "Meditation for Your Brain and Body," April 4, 2016.

xvii   meditation changes your brain: Shauna Shapiro, "How Meditation
        Changes the Brain," Greater Good Science Center video, 6:09. Posted
        June 2014; Rick Hanson, "How to Change Your Brain," Greater Good
        Science Center video, 4:06. Posted December 2013.

xvii   practicing mindfulness sitting: Ronald D. Siegel, *The Mindfulness
        Solution: Everyday Practices for Everyday Problems* (New York: Guilford
        Press, 2010).

xvii   monks' meditation practices: Christof Koch, "Neuroscientists and the
        Dalai Lama Swap Insights on Meditation," *Scientific American*, July 1,
        2013.

xvii   neuroplasticity occurred: Richard J. Davidson and Antoine Lutz,
        "Buddha's Brain: Neuroplasticity and Meditation," NIH Public Access
        Author Manuscript, *IEEE Signal Process Mag.*, September 23, 2010.

xvii   I myself sit daily: Books and tapes for mindfulness sitting are available
        from many authors. Some of my favorites are Pema Chödrön, Ronald
        Siegel, Jack Kornfield, Jon Kabat-Zinn, and Thich Nhat Hanh.

Chapter 1: WHY WE NEED A HOLISTIC ECONOMIC MODEL

4   very different criteria: Atkinson (2009); Hendren (2014).

4   to save a person's life: Peter Singer, *Famine, Affluence, and Morality* (New
        York: Oxford University Press, 2015).

4   The free market model: A. B. Atkinson, "Economics as a Moral Science,"
        Economica 76 (October 2009): 791–804; doi: 10.1111/j.1468-0335.2009
        .00788.x; Michael J. Sandel, "Market Reasoning as Moral Reasoning: Why
        Economists Should Re-engage with Political Philosophy, *Journal of Economic
        Perspectives* 27 (Fall 2013): 121–40. doi: 10.1257/jep.27.4.121.

5   morality in economics is returning: George A. Akerlof and Rachel E.
        Kranton, *Identity Economics* (Princeton: Princeton University Press,
        2011); Angus Deaton, *The Great Escape* (Princeton: Princeton University
        Press, 2015); Paul Krugman, *The Conscience of a Liberal* (New York:
        Norton, 2009) (see also his ongoing *New York Times* column); Thomas
        Piketty, *Capital in the Twenty-First Century* (Cambridge, MA: Harvard
        University Press, 2014); Wojciech Kopczuk, Emmanuel Saez, and Jae
        Song, "Earnings Inequality and Mobility in the United States: Evidence
        from Social Security Data Since 1937," *Quarterly Journal of Economics*
        125(1), 2010, 91–128; Amartya Sen, *Development as Freedom* (New York:
        Knopf, 1999); Joseph Stiglitz, *The Price of Inequality* (New York: Norton,
        2013); Anthony B. Atkinson, "Economics as a Moral Science," *Economica*,
        special issue, edited by Amos Witztum and Frank Cowell (Wiley)
        (October 2009) 76 (s1): 791–804; Sam Bowles, *The Moral Economy* (New
        Haven: Yale University Press, 2016); Jeffrey Sachs, *The Price of Civilization*
        (New York: Random House, 2012).

Chapter 2: WHAT IS BUDDHIST ECONOMICS?

7   Ideally, economics should play a part: Ven. P. A. Payutto, "Buddhist Economics: A Middle Way for the Market Place," *Urban Dharma* (1994): 3, 11.

8   Relative truths are useful in daily life: Dzongsar Khyentse Rinpoche teaching at UC Berkeley, July 19, 2015.

9   "Everything is connected to everything else": Barry Commoner, *The Closing Circle: Nature, Man, and Technology* (New York: Random House, 1971).

12   "He is happy who lives in accordance": Aristotle, *The Nicomachean Ethics*, Oxford edition. Book 10, p. 18.

12   "The contemplative life is happiest": Ibid., 193.

12   the Dalai Lama translated this: Dalai Lama, *The Art of Happiness*. The entire book is relevant. Part I provides an overview.

12   "can by itself alone": Dalai Lama, *Ethics for the New Millennium* (New York: Riverhead, 1999), 16.

12   "genuine happiness is characterized": Ibid., 99.

12   people strive to act ethically: Ibid., 61.

13   "Two Arrows Sutra": "The story of the two arrows: Physical pain is inevitable but the mental pain is optional," *Wisdom through Mindfulness* (blog), January 15, 2012.

14   Shantideva wrote: Shantideva, *The Way of the Bodhisattva* (Boulder, CO: Shambala, 2008), 16.

14   the Eightfold Path: Buddha's eightfold path is right view, right intention, right speech, right action, right livelihood, right effort, right concentration, right mindfulness. See http://buddhism.about.com/od/theeightfoldpath/a/eightfoldpath.htm.

15   Bowles argues that humans developed cooperative instincts: Samuel Bowles, *The Moral Economy: Why Good Incentive Are No Substitute for Good Citizens* (New Haven: Yale University Press, 2016), chapter 2.

17   We stop buying things: Juliet Schor, *The Overspent American: Why We Want What We Don't Need* (New York: Harper Perennial, 1999).

17   income is just one element: Buddhist economics builds upon work by development economists, notably Amartya Sen and his work on capabilities (*Development as Freedom*, Knopf, 1999), on work by ecological economists (Herman Daly), and on Buddhism as taught by Anam Thubten in *Magic of Awareness* (Snow Lion Publications, 2012). See also the excellent framework for a Buddhist economics approach in Peter Daniels, "Climate change, economics, and Buddhism—Part 1: An integrated environmental analysis framework."

20   five of the six largest companies: http://fortune.com/global500/.

20   with profit margins around 25 percent: Daniel Gilbert and Justin Scheck, "Big Oil Feels the Need to Get Smaller," *Wall Street Journal*, November 2, 2014.

22   the distribution of wealth in the world: Oxfam Research Brief, January 2015, http://www.oxfam.org/en/research/wealth-having-it-all-and-wanting-more. Based on Credit Suisse Global Wealth Databook 2014, https://www.credit-suisse.com/uk/en/news-and-expertise/research/credit-suisse-research-institute/publications.html.

22   In the United States: Emmanuel Saez and Gabriel Zucman, "Wealth Inequality in the United States Since 1913: Evidence from Capitalized Income Tax Data," National Bureau of Economic Research, October 2014.

22   Buddhist economics distinguishes: Matthews (2014).

22   The cultivation of inner wealth: "The Symbolism of the Traditional Temple," Kadampa.org, August 1, 1997.

Chapter 3: INTERDEPENDENT WITH ONE ANOTHER

24   Indra's Jewel Net: "Indra's Jewel Net: A Metaphor for Interbeing," About.com, February 25, 2016.

25   cooperation helps societies survive and grow: Samuel Bowles and Herbert Gintis, *A Cooperative Species: Human Reciprocity and Its Evolution* (Princeton: Princeton University Press, 2011).

26   what makes people happy: Keiko Otake et al., "Happy People Become Happier Through Kindness: A Counting Kindness Intervention," NIH Public Access Author Manuscript, *J Happiness Stud.*, September 2006.

26   Kindness makes you happier: Alex Dixon, "Kindness Makes You Happy . . . and Happiness Makes You Kind," Greater Good Science Center, UC Berkeley, September 6, 2011.

26   happiness comes from practicing compassion: Dalai Lama, *The Art of Happiness, 10th Anniversary Edition: A Handbook for Living* (New York: Riverhead, 2009), 22–23.

28   The Dalai Lama teaches: Ibid., 89.

29   as we figure out how to live life: Pew Research Center online, "Raising Kids and Running a Household: How Working Parents Share the Load," November 4, 2015.

30   tidying up will make us happier: Gretchen Rubin, *The Happiness Project* (New York: Harper, 2009); Marie Kondo, *The Life-Changing Magic of Tidying Up* (New York: Ten Speed Press, 2014).

30   too many choices: Barry Schwartz, *The Paradox of Choice: Why More Is Less* (New York: Harper Perennial, 2004); https://www.youtube.com/watch?v=VO6XEQIsCoM.

31   too few choices: Sendhil Mullainathan and Eldar Shafir, *Scarcity: Why Having Too Little Means So Much* (New York: Times Books, 2013).

31   The vicious cycle of poverty: Mark Bittman, "No Justice, No . . . Anything," *New York Times*, May 13, 2015.

31   In stark contrast: Christopher F. Schuetze, "Superyachts to the Rescue,"
      New York Times, January 16, 2015.

32   the Easterlin Paradox: Richard A. Easterlin et al. "The Happiness–
      Income Paradox Revisited," *Proceedings of the National Academy of Sciences
      of the United States of America,* 107.52 (2010): 22463–68. PMC. Web.
      February 9, 2015.

32   Psychologists explain this: Daniel Gilbert, *Stumbling on Happiness* (New
      York: Knopf, 2006).

33   quality of life indicators: Richard Wilkinson and Kate Pickett, *The Spirit
      Level: Why Greater Equality Makes Societies Stronger* (New York:
      Bloomsbury, 2009).

33   indicators of health and well-being have fallen: Eduardo Porter, "Income
      Inequality Is Costing the U.S. on Social Issues," *New York Times,* April
      28, 2015.

33   driven almost exclusively by excessive inequality: Alice Chen, Emily
      Oster, and Heidi Williams, "Why is Infant Mortality Higher in the US
      than in Europe?" The National Bureau of Economic Research online,
      September 2014.

33   quality of life indicators do improve with income: Richard Wilkinson
      and Kate Pickett, *The Spirit Level: Why Greater Equality Makes Societies
      Stronger* (New York: Bloomsbury, 2009).

34   relative income theory: Stevenson and Wolfers (2009) also show that
      subjective well-being measures and income are also positively related
      across countries, although Easterlin et al. (2015) do not.

34   negative consequences for individuals and society: Plato, *The Republic*
      (360 BCE), http://classics.mit.edu/Plato/republic.html.

34   only if they provide compensating benefits: Rawls, *A Theory of Justice*
      (1971, 1999).

34   Americans agree that inequality is harmful: http://www.people-press.
      org/files/legacy-questionnaires/1-23-14%20Poverty_Inequality%20
      topline%20for%20release.pdf.

34   A recent study of CEO pay: This study was based on a large data set of
      the 1,500 largest companies (by market capitalization) over the period
      1994–2013, and compared the revenues and profits of companies in
      similar fields. Susan Adams, "The Highest-Paid CEOs Are The Worst
      Performers, New Study Says," *Forbes,* June 16, 2014.

35   Distribution of income across families and country's well-being: Robert
      H. Frank, *Luxury Fever: Weighing the Cost of Excess,* (Princeton: Princeton
      University Press, 2010).

36   separated from the masses: Nelson D. Schwartz, "In an Age of Privilege,
      Not Everyone Is in the Same Boat," *New York Times,* April 23, 2016.

36   My own research analyzes: Brown, *American Standards of Living,* 1994.
      Data are from Consumer Expenditure Survey, http://www.bls.gov/cex/.

37   When inequality increases the income gap: Robert H. Frank, *Falling
      Behind: How Rising Inequality Harms the Middle Class* (University of
      California Press, 2007).

38   paid time off: Organization for Economic Co-operation and Development online, "Average annual hours actually worked per worker."

39   "Both business men and working men": Robert S. Lynd and Helen Merrell Lynd, *Middletown: A Study in Modern American Culture* (San Diego: Harcourt, 1929) 7, 87.

41   halving the 1990 extreme poverty rate: http://www.un.org/millennium goals/poverty.shtml.

41   Universal health care reduces suffering: The Lancet Commission on Global Surgery, April 28, 2015, http://www.thelancet.com/commissions /global-surgery.

42   Gross National Happiness (GNH) Index: http://www.grossnational happiness.com/.

43   the most expensive wars in U.S. history: http://www.hks.harvard.edu/ news-events/news/articles/bilmes-iraq-afghan-war-cost-wp; Blimes and Stiglitz, *The Three Trillion Dollar War: The True Cost of the Iraq Conflict* (New York: Norton, 2008); http://watson.brown.edu/costsofwar/costs.

43   In 2013, firearms were used: Jiaquan Xu, M.D., et al., "Deaths: Final Data for 2013," *National Vital Statistics Reports* 64 (February 2016).

44   moral issue of entering into war: Barbara O'Brien, "War and Buddhism," About.com.

44   "War and the large military establishments": Dailailama.com, "The Reality of War."

45   "Our collective compassion": Thich Nhat Hanh, *Love Letter to the Earth* (Berkeley, CA: Parallax Press, 2013), 69.

46   neighborhood has significant impact: Raj Chetty and Nathaniel Hendren, "The Impacts of Neighborhoods on Intergenerational Mobility," http://www.equality-of-opportunity.org/images/nbhds_exec _summary.pdf.

46   differences in economics, health, and educational outcomes: Raj Chetty, Nathaniel Hendren, and Lawrence Katz, "The Effects of Exposure to Better Neighborhoods on Children," http://www.equality-of-opportunity .org/images/mto_exec_summary.pdf.

Chapter 4: INTERDEPENDENT WITH OUR
ENVIRONMENT

49   information does not necessarily lead to behavioral change: John S. Dryzek et al., *Climate-Challenged Society* (New York: Oxford University Press, 2013).

50   Climate Change Conference in Paris (COP21): "195 countries adopt the first universal climate agreement," http://www.cop21.gouv.fr/en/195 -countries-adopt-the-first-universal-climate-agreement/.

51   The IPCC's Fifth Assessment Report (2014): http://www.ipcc.ch/.

51   fell on deaf ears: James Hansen, *Storms of My Grandchildren: The Truth About the Coming Climate Catastrophe and Our Last Chance to Save Humanity* (New York: Bloomsbury, 2009); Bill McKibben, *The End of Nature* (New York: Random House, 1989).

52   Globally, in 2010, carbon dioxide accounted: http://www3.epa.gov /climatechange/ghgemissions/global.html.

52   Another 21 percent of GHG emissions: Ibid.

53   three tons of new concrete annually: Madeleine Rubenstein, "Emissions from the Cement Industry," *State of the Planet*, Earth Institute, Columbia University blog, May 9, 2012; "Cement CO_2 Emissions," Global-greenhouse-warming.com.

53   Global warming is happening because: James Hansen, *Storms of My Grandchildren: The Truth About the Coming Climate Catastrophe and Our Last Chance to Save Humanity* (New York: Bloomsbury, 2009).

53   air pollution from black carbon: https://www3.epa.gov/blackcarbon/ basic.html.

53   human deaths from air pollution: World Health Organization online, "7 million premature deaths annually linked to air pollution," March 25, 2014.

54   hazardous levels of smog: A real-time air quality index is available online at http://aqicn.org/map/india/.

54   the world's dirtiest air: Sugam Pokharel, "This Indian city has the world's worst air," *CNN Money*, April 14, 2015.

55   carbon capture and storage (CCS): Pilita Clark, "Carbon capture: Miracle machine or white elephant?" *Financial Times*, September 9, 2015; Ian Austen, "Technology to Make Clean Energy From Coal Is Stumbling in Practice," *New York Times*, March 29, 2016.

55   carbon dioxide removal from the air: Eli Kintisch, "Sucking carbon from the sky may do little to slow climate change," *Science*, August 3, 2015.

56   the largest natural gas producer in the world: Quoctrung Bui, "U.S. Is The World's Largest Producer Of Natural Gas. Here's What That Means," *Planet Money, NPR*, October 17, 2013.

56   faster global warming than coal: http://web.stanford.edu/group/efmh/ jacobson/Articles/I/NatGasVsWWS&coal.pdf.

56   climate change is happening even faster: E. M. Fischer & R. Knutti, "Anthropogenic contribution to global occurrence of heavy-precipitation and high-temperature extremes," *Nature Climate Change* 5, 560–564 (2015). doi:10.1038/nclimate2617.

57   sea levels are rising: http://climate.nasa.gov/evidence/.

58   "Two core boundaries": Will Steffen et al., "Planetary boundaries: Guiding human development on a changing planet," *Science*, January 15, 2015, doi: 10.1126/science.1259855.

59   Glaciers are "retreating": Michael Zemp et al., "Historically unprece-dented global glacier decline in the early 21st century," *Journal*

of Glaciology 61 (September 2015): 745–62. doi: http://dx.doi
.org/10.3189/2015JoG15J017. The dataset on glacier variations includes
42,000 data points since 1600.

59   watch the glaciers disappearing: You can keep up with NASA updates at
      https://sealevel.nasa.gov/.

59   freshwater supply cannot keep pace: United Nations Environment
      Programme online, "Water withdrawal and consumption: the big gap,"
      Vital Water Graphics, http://www.unep.org/dewa/vitalwater/article42
      .html.

59   A ten-year study of global groundwater: Alexandra S. Richey et al.,
      "Quantifying renewable groundwater stress with GRACE," *Water
      Resources Research* 51 (July 2015). doi: 10.1002/2015WR017349.

60   economic losses because of drought: http://www2.epa.gov/cira.

60   the "sixth extinction": *National Geographic* online, "Mass Extinctions."

60   the current rate of extinction: Gerardo Ceballos et al., "Accelerated
      modern human-induced species loses: Entering the sixth mass extinc-
      tion," *Science Advances* (2015). doi: 10.1126/sciadv.1400253.

60   the extinction of species will accelerate: Mark C. Urban, "Accelerating
      extinction risk from climate change," *Science* 384, no. 6234 (May 2015).
      doi: 10.1126/science.aaa4984.

61   human activities spew carbon: James Hansen, *Storms of My Grandchildren:
      The Truth About the Coming Climate Catastrophe and Our Last Chance to
      Save Humanity* (New York: Bloomsbury, 2009).

61   raised the amount of CO_2: http://cdiac.ornl.gov/pns/current_ghg.html.
      For an even longer time period, see https://www3.epa.gov/climatechange
      /pdfs/print_ghg-concentrations.pdf.

61   the Anthropocene epoch: Colin N. Waters et al., "The Anthropocene is
      functionally and stratigraphically distinct from the Holocene," *Science*
      352, no. 6269 (January 2016). doi: 10.1126/science.aad2622.

62   the 2°C target: Samuel Randalls, "History of the 2 degrees C climate
      target," *WIREs Climate Change* 1 (July 2010). doi: 10.1002/wcc.62.

62   To have a 50 percent chance: Christophe McGlade and Paul Ekins, "The
      geographical distribution of fossil fuels unused when limited global
      warming to 2 °C," *Nature* 517 (January 2015). doi: 10.1038/nature14016;
      Bill McKibben, "Global Warming's Terrible New Math," *Rolling Stone*,
      July 19, 2012.

63   how the earth will evolve: Lizzie Wade, "This Is What the World Will
      Look Like After Climate Change," *Mother Jones*, September 8, 2015.

63   mitigation costs more than it's worth: Bjorn Lomborg, *Cool It: The
      Skeptical Environmentalist's Guide to Global Warming* (New York: Vintage,
      2010).

64   how humans use their ecosystems: Peter Daniels, "Climate Change,
      Economics, and Buddhism—Part 1: An Integrated Environmental
      Analysis Framework" and "Part 2: New Views and Practices for
      Sustainable World Economies," *Ecological Economics* 69 (2010) 952–72.

66   Nature's ecosystems have boundaries: Herman Daly, *Steady-State Economics*, 2nd ed. (Washington, DC: Island Press, 1991).

66   Economists have been slow: John S. Dryzek, Richard B. Norgaard, and David Schlosberg, *Climate-Challenged Society* (Oxford: Oxford University Press, 2013).

68   Nordhaus, has developed climate change policies: http://www.econ.yale.edu/~nordhaus/homepage/documents/DICE_Manual_103113r2.pdf.

68   a low or a high discount rate: Here is a simple explanation of the discount rate. In valuing an income stream over time, we "discount" future dollars to be equivalent with today's dollar. After all, if you are offered a dollar today, or a dollar in a year, you will take the dollar right now. You might be willing to take the dollar next year if it has 5 percent interest and you receive $1.05 (and you trust the offer). For this reason, the present value of a net benefit (money) stream over many years is discounted by an interest rate to calculate the net benefit in today's value. For example, if the net benefit (money stream) of a program to reduce carbon emissions is $100 annually for fifty years, the net present value is $5,000 if we do not discount future dollars; it falls to $3,920 with a 1 percent discount rate, and to $1,826 with a 5 percent discount rate.

68   Climate change models predict: IPCC Fifth Assessment Report, http://www.ipcc.ch/report/ar5/wg2/docs/WGIIAR5_SPM_Top_Level_Findings.pdf, chart on page 3.

68   Pindyck recommends using a simple analysis: Robert S. Pindyck, "Climate Change Policies: What Do the Models Tell Us?" *Journal of Economic Literature* 51 (September 2013). doi: 10.1257/jel.51.3.860.

70   "We can afford to act": Citi GPS, "Energy Darwinism II: Why a Low Carbon Future Doesn't Have to Cost the Earth," https://www.citivelocity.com/citigps/ReportSeries.action?recordId=41.

70   An *Economist* study: The Economist Intelligence Unit, "The cost of inaction: Recognising the value at risk from climate change," *The Economist*, 2015.

70   his encyclical letter *Laudato Si*: The document can be downloaded at no charge from https://s3.amazonaws.com/s3.documentcloud.org/documents/2105201/laudato-si-inglese.pdf.

72   A country's ecological footprint: The ecological footprint is the sum of all the agricultural land, forest, and fishing grounds required to produce the food and resources consumed, to absorb the wastes, and to provide space for infrastructure. http://www.footprintnetwork.org/en/index.php/GFN/; http://www.footprintnetwork.org/en/index.php/GFN/page/living_planet_report_2014_facts/. For a summary of footprint measures, see http://www.epa.gov/sustainability/analytics/environmental-footprint.htm.

72   The Dalai Lama has been expressing concern: Dalailama.com, "A Buddhist Concept of Nature."

72 relying on prayer . . . seems illogical: Associated Press, "Dalai Lama says strong action on climate change is a human responsibility," *The Guardian*, October 20, 2015.

73 Buddhist leaders from around the world: http://gbccc.org/.

73 Other prominent religious leaders: Environmental and Energy Study Institute, "Fact Sheet: Faith Organizations and Climate Change," http://www.eesi.org/papers/view/fact-sheet-faith-organizations-and-climate-change.

73 Islamic academics came together: International Islamic Climate Change Symposium, "Islamic Declaration on Global Climate Change," http://islamicclimatedeclaration.org/islamic-declaration-on-global-climate-change/.

74 U.S. military operations in the Iraq War: Mike Berners-Lee and Duncan Clark, "What's the carbon footprint of . . . the Iraq war?" *The Guardian*, July 8, 2010.

74 "the world's most fearsome weapon of mass destruction": Matthew Lee, "Climate change world's 'most fearsome' weapon of mass destruction: Kerry," *CTV News*, February 16, 2014.

74 What you eat makes a big difference: Oxford study based on British diets, Peter Scarborough et al., "Dietary greenhouse gas emissions of meat-eaters, fish-eaters, vegetarians and vegans in the UK," *Climatic Change* (2014). doi: 10.1007/s10584-014-1169-1.

74 what kind of meat you eat: Gidon Eshel et al., "Land, irrigation water, greenhouse gas, and reactive nitrogen burdens of meat, eggs, and dairy production in the United States," *PNAS* 111 (February 2014). doi: 10.1073/pnas.1402183111.

76 "Caring about the environment": Thich Nhat Hanh, *Love Letter to the Earth* (Berkeley, CA: Parallax Press, 2013), 82.

77 industrialized countries are responsible: Clark, Duncan, "Which nations are most responsible for climate change?" The ultimate climate challenge FAQ, *The Guardian*, April 21, 2011.

78 top five greenhouse gas emitters: Calculated from World Resources Institute CAIT Climate Data Explorer: Historic Emissions. http://cait.wri.org/.

78 CO_2 emissions per person: Calculated from: Clark, Duncan, "Which nations are most responsible for climate change?" The ultimate climate challenge FAQ, *The Guardian*, April 21, 2011.

79 More than half the vehicles sold in 2014: Mike Ramsey, "Tesla Presses Its Case on Fuel Standards," *Wall Street Journal*, August 2, 2015.

79 how temperature affects productivity: Marshall Burke and Solomon M. Hsian et el., "Global non-linear effect of temperature on economic production," *Nature* 527 (November 2015). doi: 10.1038/nature15725.

80 developing resilient systems: http://sixfoundations.org/.

80 the 2015 COP21 agreement: The text of the agreement may be found at http://www.cop21.gouv.fr/wp-content/uploads/2015/12/l09r01.pdf.

81   The agreement acknowledges the harm: Coral Davenport et al., "Inside the Paris Climate Deal," *The New York Times*, December 12, 2015.

81   climate change calculator: http://ig.ft.com/sites/climate-change-calculator/. Another, more detailed calculator for the planet is available at http://tool .globalcalculator.org/globcalc.html?levers=22rfoe2e13be1111c2c2c1n31hfjdc ef222hp233f211111fn2211111111/dashboard/en.

82   global warming costs: These figures are in 2013 U.S. dollars. http://web .stanford.edu/group/efmh/jacobson/Articles/I/CountriesWWS.pdf.

82   Clean Power Plan: http://www.epa.gov/cleanpowerplan/clean-power -plan-existing-power-plants.

Chapter 5: PROSPERITY FOR BOTH RICH AND POOR

84   We are resolved to free the human race: United Nations Sustainable Development Knowledge Platform online, "Transforming out world: the 2030 Agenda for Sustainable Development."

85   as we share resources globally: Anthony B. Atkinson (2012), "Public Economics After the Idea of Justice," *Journal of Human Development and Capabilities* 13 (July 2012), 521–36. doi: 10.1080/19452829.2012 .703171.

86   interferes with global markets and might support corruption: See, for example, H. Doucouliagos and M. Paldam, "Conditional Aid Effectiveness: A Meta-Analysis," *Journal of International Development*, 21 (January 2009): 1582–1601.

86   Global wealth is concentrated: Oxfam Research Brief, "Wealth: Having It All and Wanting More," Oxfam.org, January 2015. Based on the Forbes billionaires list 2002–2014, http://www.forbes.com /billionaires/.

87   protect their profits and lower their taxes: Ibid.

87   a modest decline in global inequality: Globalinequality (blog), "National vices, global virtue: Is the world becoming more equal?" December 22, 2014. Data for 2011, 2008, and 1988.

88   inequality of income within most countries has grown: Oxfam International online, "Working for the Few: Political capture and economic inequality," January 2014.

87   Let's make the point even stronger: Oxfam International online, "Income of richest 100 people enough to end poverty four times over," January 18, 2013. The UN defined extreme poverty as income of or below $1.25 per day in 2005 international dollars.

88   inequality is not an inherent outcome of capitalism: Joseph Stiglitz, *The Price of Inequality: How Today's Divided Society Endangers Our Future* (New York: Norton, 2013).

88   a list of national regulations: Tina Rosenberg, "Guiding a First Generation
        to College," Opinionator, *New York Times*, April 26, 2016.
89   equality is a choice driven by government policies: Robert J. Shiller,
        "Better Insurance Against Inequality," *New York Times*, April 12, 2014.
90   Atkinson proposes the adoption of fifteen policies: Anthony B. Atkinson,
        Inequality (Cambridge, MA: Harvard University Press, 2015).
90   raising minimum wages in California: M. Reich et al. "Minimum Wages
        Across State Borders," *Review of Economics and Statistics* (2010).
90   *average* incomes across countries: Wikipedia, "List of countries by GDP
        (PPP) per capita," accessed March 6, 2016. The extreme poverty
        threshold is adjusted when world prices are recalculated. See Francisco
        Ferreira, "The international poverty line has just been raised to $1.90 a
        day, but global poverty is basically unchanged. How is that even
        possible?" Worldbank.org, October 4, 2015.
91   coordinated effort can pay off: United Nations Department of Economic
        and Social Affairs online, "The Millennium Development Goals Report
        2015."
92   the Five P's: United Nations Sustainable Development Knowledge
        Platform,   https://sustainabledevelopment.un.org/content/documents
        /7891Transforming%20Our%20World.pdf.
92   On the negative side: Jeffrey Sachs, *The Age of Sustainable Development*
        (New York: Columbia University Press, 2014), analyzes seven reasons
        why countries are poor.
3   top-down technocratic approach: William Easterly, *The Tyranny of
        Experts: Economists, Dictators, and the Forgotten Rights of the Poor* (New
        York: Basic Books, 2014).
93   official aid to the developing world: UN Millennium Project, "The 0.7%
        target: An in-depth look," http://www.unmillenniumproject.org/press
        /07.htm.
94   brunt of the damage from global warming: United Nations Development
        Programme, *Human Development Report 2007/2008*, UNDP.org.
94   deteriorating quality of life . . . and health problems: Nick Watts et al.,
        "Health and climate change: policy responses to protect public health,"
        The Lancet 386 (November 2015). doi: http://dx.doi.org/10.1016/S0140
        -6736(15)60854-6.
95   Luke Mills and Angus McCrone, "Clean Energy Investment by the
        Numbers—End of Year 2015," https://www.bnef.com/dataview/clean-
        energy-investment/index.html.
95   Here are the shocking numbers: Carbon emissions (for 2013) from PBL
        Netherlands Environmental Assessment Agency, "Trends in Global
        CO_2 Emissions: 2014 Report," http://edgar.jrc.ec.europa.eu/news_docs/jrc
        -2014-trends-in-global-co2-emissions-2014-report-93171.pdf; GDP and
        population (2015) from https://en.wikipedia.org/wiki/World_economy.
95   Disparities among countries are large: Oxfam Media Briefing, "Extreme
        Carbon Inequality," December 2, 2015, Oxfam.org.

96   GHG emissions are slowly becoming decoupled: Nate Aden, "The
      Roads to Decoupling: 21 Countries Are Reducing Carbon Emissions
      While Growing GDP," World Resources Institute, April 5, 2016, World
      Resources Institute (blog).

97   "To resist the excesses of consumerism": Jeffrey D. Sachs, *The Price of
      Civilization: Reawakening American Virtue and Prosperity* (New York:
      Random House, 2012), chapter 1, page 10.

98   sustainable consumption and production (SCP) goal: United Nations,
      "Sustainable Development Goals: 17 Goals to Transform Our World,"
      UN.org.

99   the world's financial markets: Joseph E. Stiglitz, "America in the Way,"
      Columbia University Committee on Global Thought, August 6, 2015,
      http://cgt.columbia.edu/news/stiglitz-america-in-the-way/.

100   Undertaken by Greece austerity actions: Trading Economics online,
      "Greece Youth Unemployment Rate."

100   As wages and incomes fell: Joseph Stiglitz et al., "In the final hour, a
      plea for economic sanity and humanity," *Financial Times*, Letters, June 5,
      2015.

100   rebelling against the global financial sector: Paul Krugman, "Ending
      Greece's Nightmare," *New York Times*, January 26, 2015; "The
      Conscience of a Liberal" *New York Times*, July 10, 2015.

101   The current Syrian civil war: Jeffrey D. Sachs, "Ending the Syrian War,"
      Project Syndicate, February 29, 2016.

101   influx of people: The UNHCR website provides data and analysis of
      displaced persons around the world: http://www.unhcr.org/pages
      /5694d22b6.html.

101   "Do not come to Europe": James Kanter and Sewell Chan, "Europe,
      Reeling from Strain, Tells Economic Migrants: Don't Bother," *New York
      Times*, March 3, 2016.

101   the admission of refugees into their states: Ashley Fantz and Ben
      Brumfield, "More than half the nation's governors say Syrian refugees
      not welcome," *CNN*, November 19, 2015.

101   The billionaire financier and philanthropist: George Soros, "Rebuilding
      the Asylum System," *Project Syndicate*, September 26, 2015.

Chapter 6: MEASURING QUALITY OF LIFE

107   GDP does have several things going for it: Diana Coyle, *GDP: A Brief
      but Affectionate History* (Princeton: Princeton University Press, 2014);
      Dirk Philipsen, *The Little Big Number: How GDP Came to Rule the World
      and What to Do About It* (Princeton: Princeton University Press, 2015);
      Philipp Lepenies, *The Power of a Single Number* (New York: Columbia
      University Press, 2016).

III   Using the GNH: http://www.grossnationalhappiness.com; see detailed
       2010 survey report at http://www.grossnationalhappiness.com/wp
       -content/uploads/2012/04/Short-GNH-Index-edited.pdf.

III   Human Development Index (HDI): In 2010 two inequality indices were
       created. The IHDI adjusts HDI for inequality in a country's distribution
       of each of the three dimensions, and the Gender Inequality Index (GII)
       measures inequality in achievements between women and men in repro-
       ductive health, empowerment and labor market participation. See http://
       hdr.undp.org/en/data for 2014.

113   To measure and compare the quality of life in rich countries: fig. 3 (2005
       U.S. dollars) in Kubiszewski et al., "Beyond GDP: Measuring and
       Achieving Global Genuine Progress," *Ecological Economics* September
       2013, Sciencedirect.com.

116   *hedonic happiness*: Here we will use "hedonic happiness" to mean *subjective
       well-being*, or how people self-report feeling about their own lives, such as
       feelings of pain or pleasure, of life satisfaction, of "best possible" or
       "worst possible" life. Subjective well-being has a large literature (see
       National Research Council, "Subjective Well-Being," 2013).

117   "capabilities for the miserable; happiness for the satisfied": Jose M.
       Edwards and Sophie Pelle, "Capabilities for the Miserable; Happiness for
       the Satisfied," *Journal of the History of Economic Thought*, 33 (September
       2011). doi: 10.1017/S1053837211000216.

117   that measure is influenced by culture: James R. Lincoln and Arne L.
       Kalleberg, *Culture, Control, and Commitment: A Study of Work Organization
       and Work Attitudes in the U.S. and Japan* (Cambridge: Cambridge
       University Press, 1990).

118   the Cantril Ladder does show a wide range: World Happiness Report
       2016, figure 2.2 and table 2.1, http://worldhappiness.report/ed/2016/.

118   how happiness is distributed: Only the Middle East and North Africa
       were more unequal (0.26). United Nations online, *World Happiness Report
       2013*, http://unsdsn.org, fig. 2.8.

119   average life satisfaction score between 6.5 and 7.5: OECD Better
       Life Index, http://www.oecdbetterlifeindex.org/topics/life-satisfaction/.
       Average happiness was between 6.5 and 7.5 for 23 countries, between 5.6
       and 6.1 for 8 countries, and between 4.8 and 5.1 for 3 countries.

119   per capita income is much more spread out: Income in PPP 2010 U.S.
       dollars, http://stats.oecd.org/Index.aspx?DataSetCode=PDB_LV.

119   inequality of happiness varies across countries: *World Happiness Report*,
       2016, Chapter 2, http://worldhappiness.report/ed/2016/.

119   We can measure the distribution of happiness: Calculated from the
       Economist Online, "Inequality and happiness: I dream of Gini," October
       12, 2011.

120   how a country's happiness score changes over time: Carol Graham,
       *Happiness Around the World: The Paradox of Happy Peasants and Miserable
       Millionaires* (Oxford: Oxford University Press, 2012).

121   Some surveys ask people: Diener's Psychological Well-Being Scale, January 2009, includes both questions (out of eight suggested questions to measure eudaimonic happiness).

122   we turn to the Happy Planet Index (HPI): http://www.happyplanet index.org/about/. Click on "explore the data" and then download the HPI 2016 dataset and the Methods paper, which are used for my explanations and calculations in this section. HPI 2016 is based on data from 2012, and adjusts both life expectancy and the Cantril Ladder for inequality using the Atkinson Index. The calculation of the HDI includes specific adjustments and scaling, and the final HPI can range between 0 and 100. Do not rely on the Briefing paper, which is somewhat misleading.

122   Rich countries do well: all country data are from the "Complete HPI data" tab and the "Rank Order" tab of the HPI 2016 dataset. Jeffrey, K., Wheatley, H., Abdallah, S. (2016). The Happy Planet Index: 2016. A global index of sustainable well-being. London: New Economics Foundation.

122   they tell us that the planet is not happy: The sustainable ecological footprint per person of 1.73 is based on 2012 data, when world population was a little over 7 billion. The sustainable footprint declines below 1.73 as world population continues to increase, expected to reach 9 billion by 2050. https://esa.un.org/unpd/wpp/Graphs/Probabilistic/POP/TOT/.

123   Both China and India have large numbers of extremely poor: calculated from Goal 1, United Nations Department of Economic and Social Affairs online, "The Millennium Development Goals Report 2014." Data for 2010.

123   the Genuine Progress Indicator: The GPI follows the approach used by the Index of Sustainable Economic Welfare (ISEW), H. Daly and J. Cobb, *For the Common Good* (Boston: Beacon Press, 1989), and the original study by Nordhaus and Tobin, "Measurement of Economic Welfare," 1972. For more details, see http://genuineprogress.net /genuine-progress-indicator/.

124   National GPI has been estimated: Ida Kubiszewski et al, "Beyond GDP: Measuring and achieving global genuine progress," *Ecological Economics* 93 (2013) 57–68. For GPI data on U.S. states, see http://utpop.transition saltlake.org/wp-content/uploads/2014/11/Utah_GPI__Report_v74_ withabstract.pdf.

126   the OECD Better Life Index: http://www.oecdbetterlifeindex.org/. You can go online and calculate your own aggregated BLI: plug in your rating of importance for each indicator, from 0 (low) to 5 (high), and then the program provides a single-value BLI for the OECD countries.

126   no aggregation of the indicators: The BLI normalizes each variable by first finding the maximum and minimum average values for the 36 countries in its sample, and then dividing the difference between a country's average and minimum values by the difference between the maximum

and minimum values. After individual variables are normalized, the BLI aggregates them to the 11 indicators by using a simple average (equal weights). The min-max values vary by the year, and possibly by the sample. Change in indicators cannot be compared across years.

128   The UK Well-Being Measures: The National Archives Office for National Statistics, "Measuring National Well-being," http://www.ons. gov.uk/ons/guide-method/user-guidance/well-being/index.html; interactive wheel: http://www.neighbourhood.statistics.gov.uk/HTML Docs/dvc146/wrapper.html.

128   Another measurement system is now in the works: United Nations Sustainable Development Solutions Network, "Preliminary Sustainable Development Goal Index and Dashboard," http://unsdsn.org/resources /publications/sdg-index/. This is a preliminary report. Look online for final reports.

Chapter 7: LEAP TO BUDDHIST ECONOMICS

133   We need markets that provide incentives: Anatole Kaletsky, *Capitalism 4.0* (New York: Bloomsbury, 2010).

134   focusing only on the next business or political cycle: Bank of England online, "Breaking the tragedy of the horizon—climate change and financial stability—speech by Mark Carney," September 29, 2015.

134   a carbon tax is required: Christine Lagarde and Jim Yong Kim, "The Path to Carbon Pricing," *Project Syndicate*, October 19, 2015.

135   phase out their fossil fuel subsidies: Organisation for Economic Co-operation and Development online, "OECD Companion to the Inventory of Support Measures for Fossil Fuels 2015," September 21, 2015.

135   direct fossil fuel subsidies: David Coady et al., "How Large Are Global Energy Subsidies?" *IMF Working Papers* (May 2015), http://www.imf. org/external/pubs/ft/wp/2015/wp15105.pdf.

136   One inclusive program is "cap and dividend": Peter Barnes, *With Liberty and Dividends for All* (San Francisco: Berrett-Koehler, 2014); http:// dividendsforall.net/.

136   this plan would generate a $5,000 dividend: Dividends for All, "PotentialRevenueSources," http://dividendsforall.net/potential-revenue-sources/.

136   The observed reduction in air pollutants: Joseph S. Shapiro and Reed Walker, "Why is Pollution from U.S. Manufacturing Declining?" (September 2015), http://faculty.haas.berkeley.edu/rwalker/research /ShapiroWalkerPollutionProductivityTrade.pdf.

137   Robert Reich advocates a version of this program: Robert Reich, *Saving Capitalism* (New York: Knopf, 2015).

137   a capital endowment to young people: Atkinson, *Inequality* (Cambridge: Harvard University Press, 2015). Hamilton and Darity propose a similar program for those born into poverty: "Can 'Baby Bonds' Eliminate the Racial Wealth Gap in Putative Post-Racial America?" *The Review of Black Political Economy* 37 (October 2010) doi: 10.1007/s12114-010-9063-1.

137   The companies then benefit: Joseph Blasi el al., *The Citizen's Share: Putting Ownership Back into Democracy* (New Haven: Yale University Press, 2014).

138   "Keep it in the ground": http://www.ecoshiftconsulting.com/blog /ecoshift-study-ending-new-federal-fossil-fuel-leases-would-keep-450-billion-tons-of-carbon-pollution-in-the-ground/.

140   *Energiewende*: http://www.claudiakemfert.de/fileadmin/user_upload/pdf /pdf_publikationen/DIW_kompakt_2015.pdf.

140   The wind, water, and sunlight (WWS) roadmap: http://web. stanford.edu/group/efmh/jacobson/Articles/I/susenergy2030.html.

140   Deep Decarbonization Pathways Project: http://deepdecarbonization. org/; conversion from 2010 baseline to 1990 baseline done with data from http://cdiac.ornl.gov/ftp/ndp030/global.1751_2011.ems.

141   the path to zero emissions: See Sustainable Development Solutions Network, *Pathways to Deep Decarbonization*, September 2015, figure 1. http://deepdecarbonization.org/wp-content/uploads/2015/12/DDPP_ EXESUM-1.pdf.

141   module prices fell 20 to 30 percent: International Renewable Energy Agency online, "Solar Photovoltaics," June 2012, http://www.irena. org/.

142   do not always bring about the expected results: *Planet Energy News* online, "Carbon capture: Miracle machine or white elephant?" September 13, 2015.

142   Generation 4 nuclear energy methods: World Nuclear Association online, "Generation IV Nuclear Reactors," July 2016.

142   Fast reactors, in particular: James Hansen, *Storms of My Grandchildren: The Truth About the Coming Climate Catastrophe and Our Last Chance to Save Humanity* (New York: Bloomsbury, 2009).

143   the substantially lower amount of $61.8 billion: OECD online, "Climate Finance in 2013-14 and the USD 100 billion goal," (2015).

144   GDP per person lags considerably: 2014 GDP per capita (PPP international dollars), http://data.worldbank.org/indicator/NY.GDP.PCAP. PP.CD.

144   its new investments in coal-fired plants: http://www.claudiakemfert.de /fileadmin/user_upload/pdf/pdf_publikationen/Heinrich_Bo__ll_ Stiftung_decoupling.pdf.

144   zero or negative population growth: Matt Rosenberg, "Negative Population Growth: 20 Countries Have Negative or Zero Natural Increase," About.com, About Education (blog), July 22, 2016.

145   70 percent of soybeans worldwide: United Soybean Board online, "U.S. soy farmers poised for growth in global animal-feed industry," January 26, 2011, http://unitedsoybean.org/.

146   Sustainable agriculture practices: http://www.ucsusa.org/our-work /food-agriculture/our-failing-food-system/industrial-agriculture#. Vjehn_lVikp.

146   rural ecosystems: R. M. Aggarwal, "Globalization, Local Ecosystems, and the Rural Poor," *World Development* 34 (August 2006), 1405–18. doi:10.1016/j.worlddev.2005.10.011.

148   If food waste were a country: Food and Agriculture Organization of the United Nations, "Cutting food waste to feed the world," May 11, 2011, http://www.fao.org/news/story/en/item/74192/icode/.

149   "The epidemic of obesity": William H. Dietz, "The Response of the US Centers for Disease Control and Prevention to the Obesity Epidemic," *Annual Review of Public Health* 36 (March 2015): 575–96. doi: 10.1146/ annurev-publhealth-031914-122415.

149   attempts to tax soft drinks: Press Association, "'Sugar tax' needed to curb childhood obesity, say experts," *The Guardian*, June 22, 2014.

149   The soft drink companies won: Matt Drange, "Soda Industry Pours Millions into Campaign to Defeat Richmond Tax," *NBC Bay Area* online, November 2, 2012.

151   Wealth Accounting and Valuation of Ecosystem Services: http://www. wavespartnership.org/en/about-us.

153   Economists for Peace and Security: http://www.epsusa.org. You can read short articles in their free newsletter at http://www.epsusa.org /publications/newsletter/newsletter.htm.

153   excellent research by world-renowned scholars: Some of the same econ- omists publish their work on how to deal constructively with conflict and climate change at www.project-syndicate.org, "the world's opinion page." Although many sides of issues are presented, those that reflect Buddhist economics are easy to spot.

153   The global arms trade: Stockholm International Peace Research Institute online, "International arms transfers," http://www.sipri.org/.

154   Saudi Arabia dramatically increased its weapons imports: Niall McCarthy, "Saudi Arabia Has Become The World's Biggest Arms Importer," *Forbes*, March 10, 2015.

154   the landmark Arms Trade Treaty (ATT): United Nations Office for Disarmament Affairs Treaties Database Home, "Arms Trade Treaty," http://disarmament.un.org/treaties/t/att.

155   Working Assets (now Credo): http://workingassets.com/Recipients. aspx.

155   Working Assets (now Credo) in the United States: http://www.interface .com/US/en-US/about/mission/Our-Mission.

156   graduate students at Berkeley who developed and deployed new technologies: http://deveng.berkeley.edu/.

156   social entrepreneurship: For example: Brent Freeman, "5 Great Companies That Make Money & Do Good," *Inc.*, August 16, 2012; Social Enterprise World Forum 2015, "Social Enterprises from the World: A Deep and Enduring Social Impact," http://sewf2015.org /social-enterprises-a-deep-and-enduring-social-impact/.

157   A Harvard Business School study: Robert G. Eccles et al., "The Impact of Corporate Sustainability on Organizational Processes and Performance," http://www.hbs.edu/faculty/Publication%20Files/SSRN-id1964011 _6791edac-7daa-4603-a220-4a0c6c7a3f7a.pdf.

157   information and tool kits: World Resources Institute, "Business," http:// www.wri.org/our-work/topics/business.

157   "physical risks, such as claims from floods and storms": Larry Elliott, "Carney warns of risks from climate change 'tragedy of the horizon,'" *The Guardian*, September 29, 2015.

157   Another study done at the London School of Economics: Simon Dietz et al., "'Climate value at risk' of global financial assets," *Nature Climate Change* (April 2016). doi:10.1038/nclimate2972.

158   Large insurers are pushing: Ken Silverstein, "Rift Widening Between Energy and Insurance Industries Over Climate Chance," *Forbes*, May 18, 2014.

158   the private sector has responded: CDP North America online, "Climate Action and Profitability: CDP S&P 500 Climate Change Report 2014," https://www.cdp.net/.

158   a global initiative called RE100: http://there100.org/companies.

158   The White House brought together: The White House Office of the Press Secretary, "FACT SHEET: White House Announces Commitments to the American Business Act on Climate Pledge," Whitehouse.gov., October 19, 2015.

158   A plenitude of sources exist: http://laszlo-zsolnai.net/content/frontiers-business-ethics; http://www.sustainablevaluepartners.com/.

159   Corporate social responsibility (CSR): Geoffrey M. Heal, "Corporate Social Responsibility—An Economic and Financial Framework," (December 2004). doi: 10.2139/ssrn.642762; Amy J. Hillman et al., "Shareholder Value, Stakeholder Management, and Social Issues: What's the Bottom Line?" *Strategic Maangement Journal*, 22 (February 2001), 125–139.

159   "circular production": William McDonough et al., *The Upcycle* (New York: North Point Press, 2013).

160   The divestment movement: http://gofossilfree.org/; http://divestinvest. org/.

162   earnings gap between executives and other earners: Natalie Sabadish and Lawrence Mishel, "CEO pay and the top 1%," *Economic Policy Institute* online, May 2, 2012.

162   companies using human-centered strategies: Zeynep Ton, *The Good Job Strategy* (Amazon Publishing, 2014). http://zeynepton.com/book/.

164   Buddhist Declaration on Climate Change: Ecological Buddhism, "A
       Buddhist Declaration on Climate Change," http://www.ecobuddhism.
       org/bcp/all_content/buddhist_declaration, 2015.

167   "The healing of our bodies and minds": Thich Nhat Hanh, *Love Letter to
       the Earth* (Berkeley, CA: Parallax Press, 2013), 240, 572, 627.

168   a relentless and popular campaign: Bill McKibben, "Exxon, Keystone,
       and the Turn Against Fossil Fuels," *New Yorker*, November 6, 2015.

168   Climate Action Network (CAN): http://www.climatenetwork.org
       /campaigns.

169   spread lies and misleading information: Robert Brulle, "America has
       been duped on climate change," *Washington Post*, January 6, 2016.

169   the path taken by the tobacco companies: Oreskes and Conway, *Merchants
       of Doubt* (New York: Bloomsbury, 2011).

169   investigate whether Exxon violated the law: John Schwartz, "Pressure
       on Exxon Over Climate Change Intensifies with New Documents,"
       New York Times, April 14, 2016; Kate Sheppard, "DOJ Sends Request for
       Exxon Probe to the FBI," *Huffington Post*, March 3, 2016; Bob Simison,
       "New York Attorney General Subpoenas Exxon on Climate Research,"
       Inside Climate News, November 5, 2015.

171   "As social animals we need love and compassion": Dalailama.com, "Basic
       Human Nature is Compassion: His Holiness the Dalai Lama Talks to
       Students at Kalindi College," January 29, 2015.

INDEX

Note: page numbers followed by *f* refer to figures.

and black carbon emissions, 53–54
and climate change, action on,
     94–96, 95, 96, 141, 143–44
obligation to help, 32, 95, 143–45

Easterlin Paradox, 32–33, 104
ecological footprint
individual, reduction of, 76–77, 98
of rich countries, 122–23
and sustainability, 71–72
economic performance measures for
     Buddhist economics
dashboards, 110, 112, 126–28, 130,
     150–51
existing models for, 106, 129–30
factors included in, 103–6, 108–9
and happiness measures, 116–21
as holistic, 105–6, 109–12
need for, 129–30
nondollar indices, 110–12
nonmarket activities in, 105
quality of life measures, 112–16,
     124–28
and realignment of policy goals,
     106
as reflection of values, 103
single-value measures, 110
sustainability measures, 122–23,
     149–52
UN-GPI as, 150–52
economics, and morality, 5, 21
Eightfold Path, 14, 15
energy policy, in Buddhist vs. free
     market economics, 19–21
environmental, social and governance
     (ESG) factors, in investing,
     160
environmental concerns
in Buddhist economics, 9, 10, 18
in free market economics, xi, 9–10,
     63–64
public apathy on, xii
range of threats, xi–xii
regulations, effectiveness of, 136
and weak vs. strong sustainability
     models, 10, 65–66, 125–26
environmental groups, 168
ethanol, 56

financial markets, global,
     mismanagement of, 99–100

food
and obesity, 149
and sustainability, 74–76, 75f,
     145–46, 166–67
wasting of, 148–49
fossil fuel companies
and climate change debate, 67, 69,
     168–69
subsidies for, 134–35
fossil fuels
and climate change, 48–49, 61, 62,
     63, 78
environmental degradation from, 51
free market vs. Buddhist economics
     on, 20
and sustainability, 105
taxing and regulation of, 20–21, 64,
     68–69, 134–37
transition to renewable energy, 82,
     138–43
use of, as choice, xiii
Four Noble Truths, 14–15
fracking, 56, 138–39
Francis (Pope), 70–71, 73
free market economics
cost-benefit approach to
     environment, xi, 9–10,
     63–64
on human nature, x–xi, 15
as inadequate to current needs,
     viii–ix
on income inequality, 34–35
and inequality, ignoring of, 2, 3, 4
influence of, 4, 5, 97
on market efficiency, 2–3, 4–5
priorities in, ix, x–xi, 1–2, 3, 12, 20
suffering created by, 18
underlying assumptions in, ix
zero-sum approach in, 3–4, 24–25
free markets
exclusion of poor from, 3
as fiction, 40, 133

GDP (gross domestic product), as
     economic measure, 104–5,
     107–8, 129
Genuine Progress Indicator (GPI), 106,
     110, 115–16, 124–26, 129–30,
     150. See also UN-GPI
geoengineering, 54–55
Gini coefficient, 88–90, 89f, 118

A NOTE ON THE AUTHOR

CLAIR BROWN is a professor of economics and the director of the Center for Work, Technology, and Society at the University of California, Berkeley. An economist focusing on work and economic justice, she is a past director of the Institute of Industrial Relations at Berkeley and past chair of the Committee on Education Policy of the UCB Academic Senate.